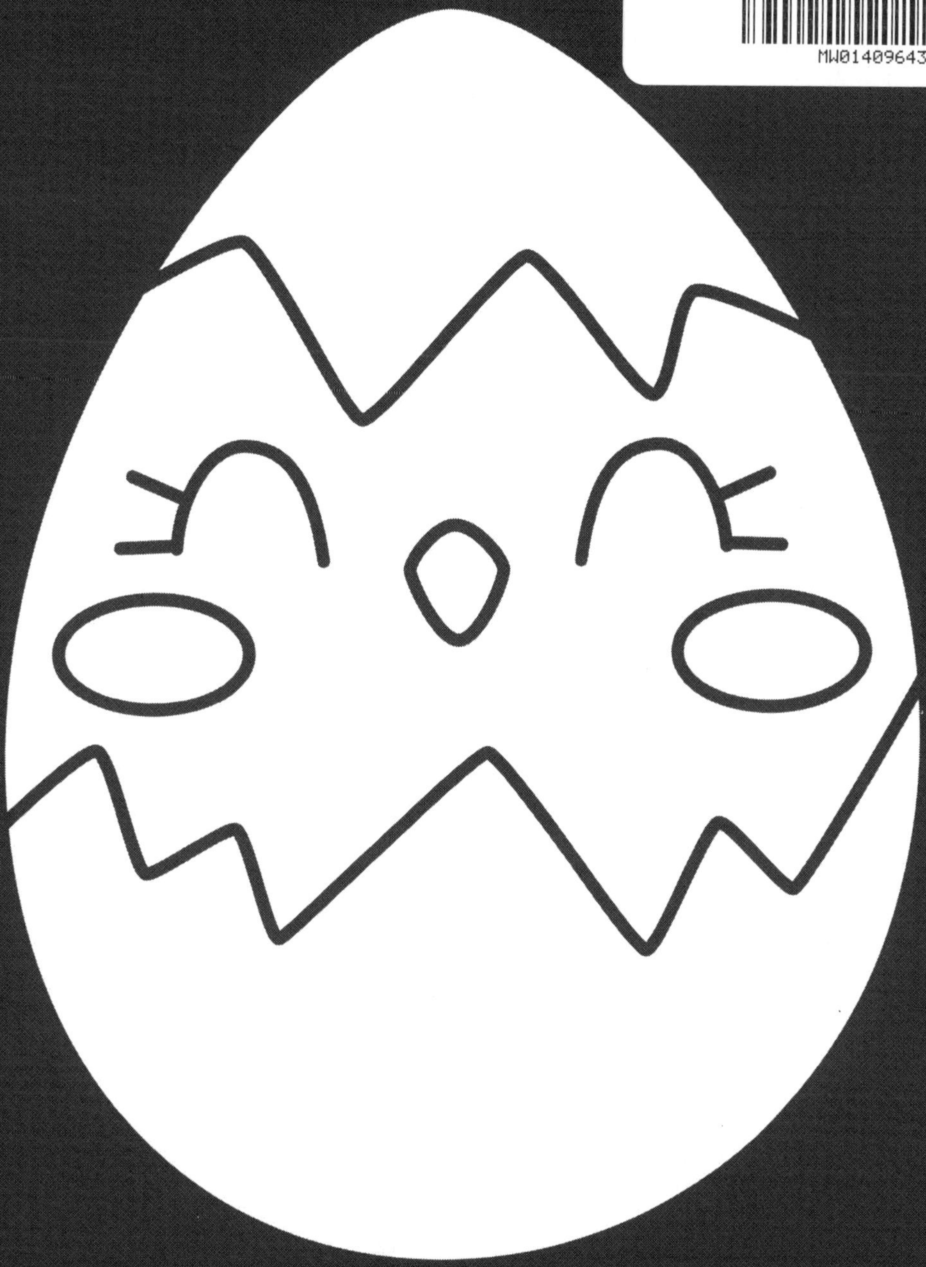

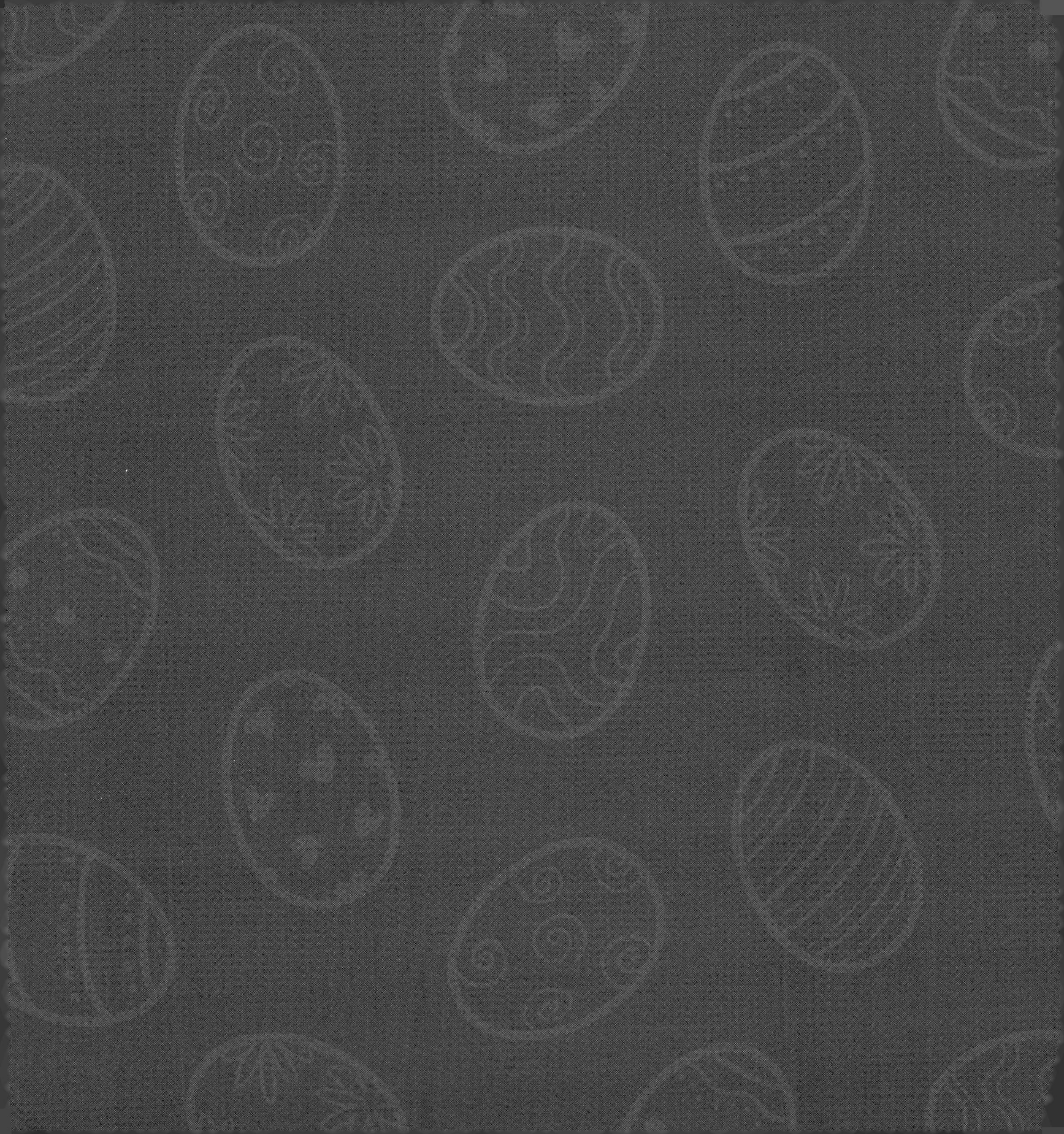

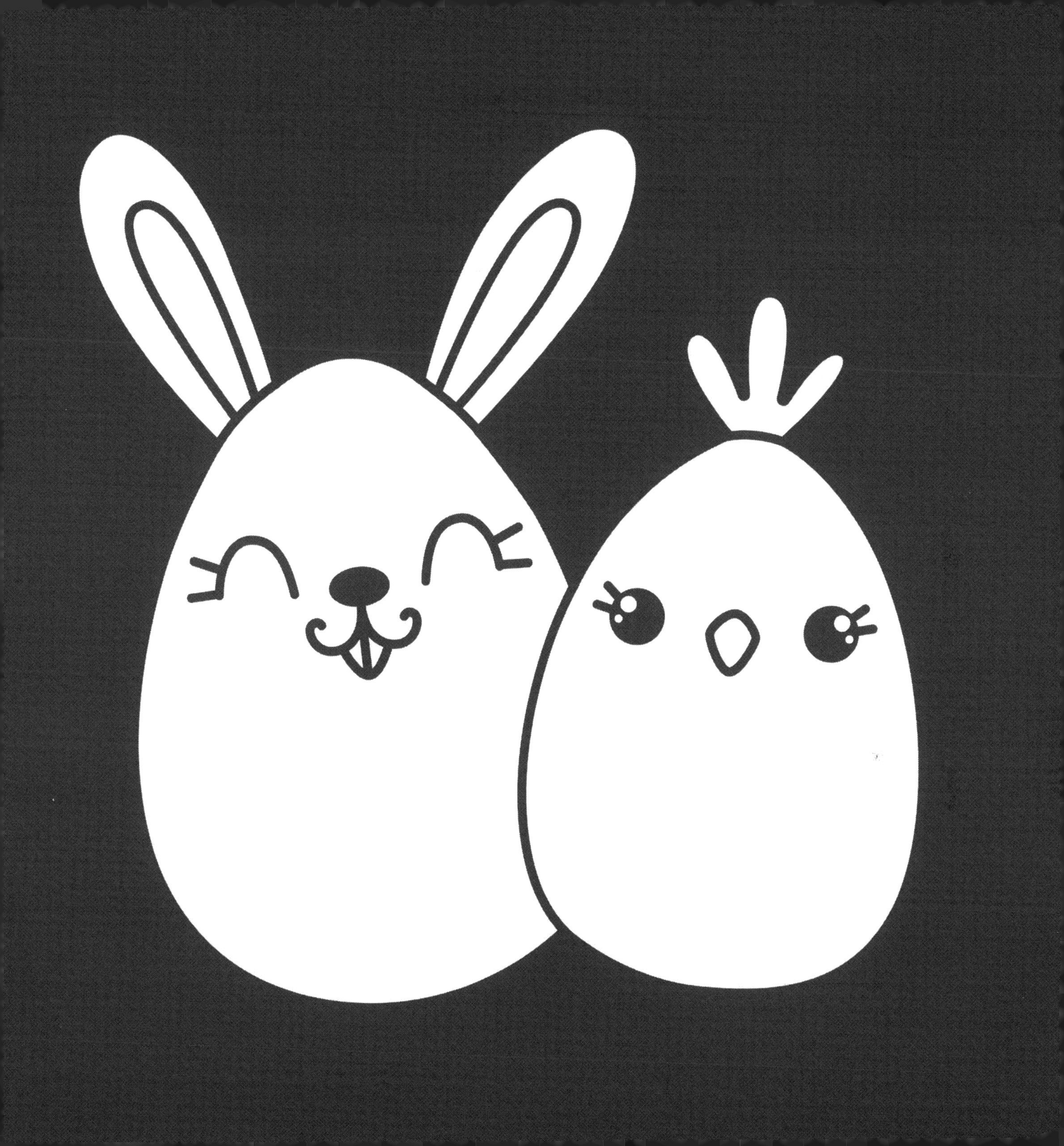

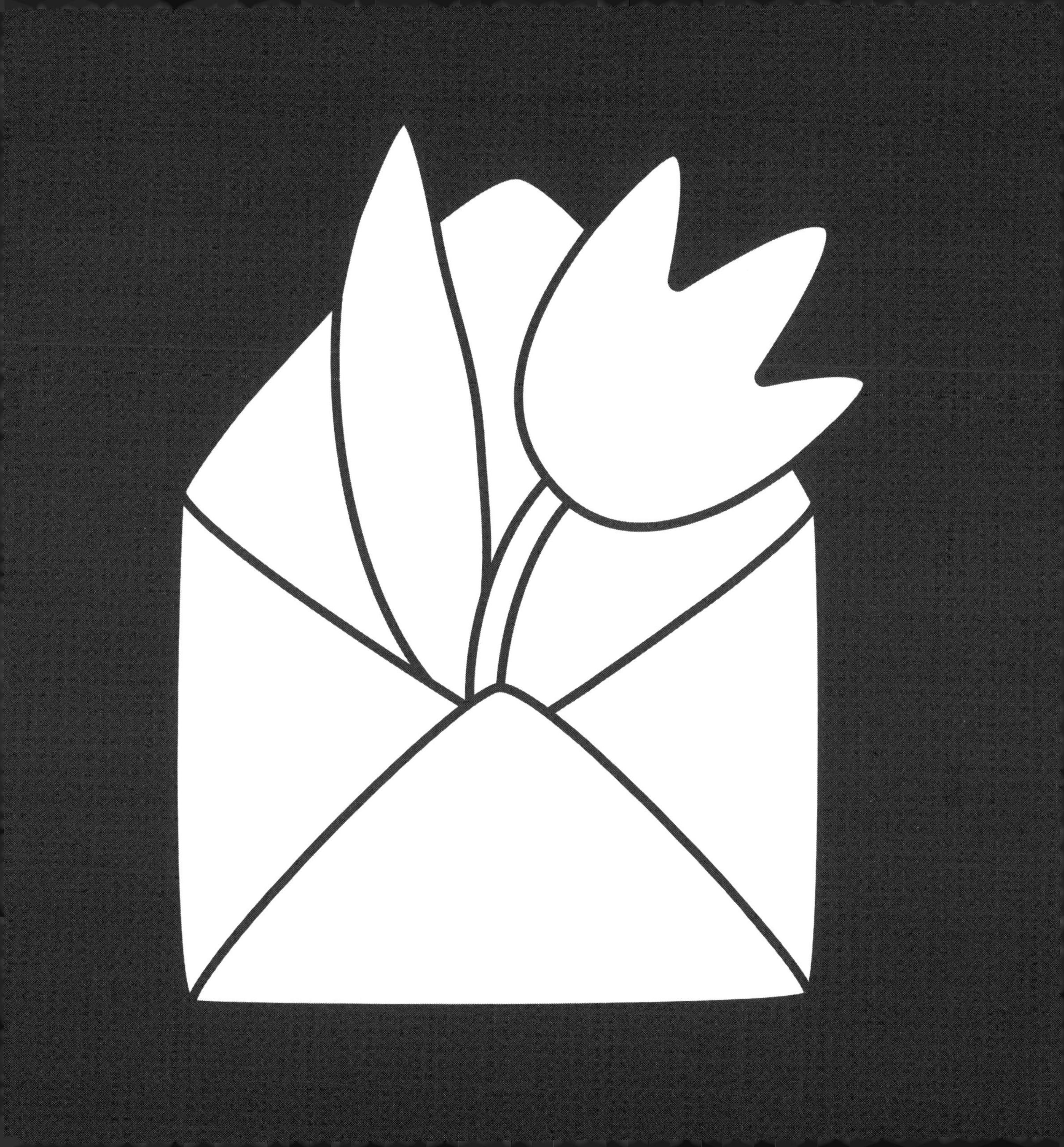

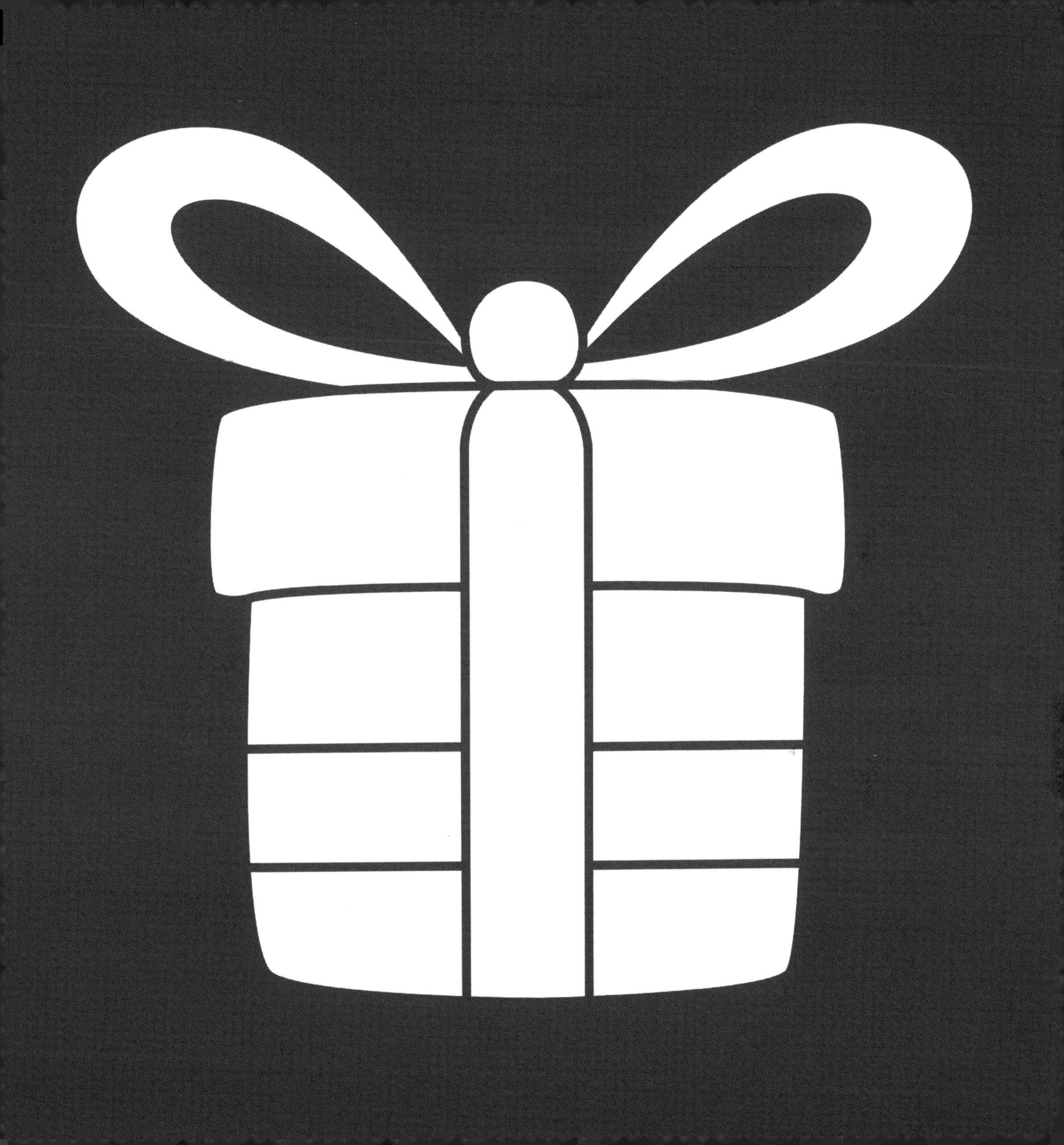

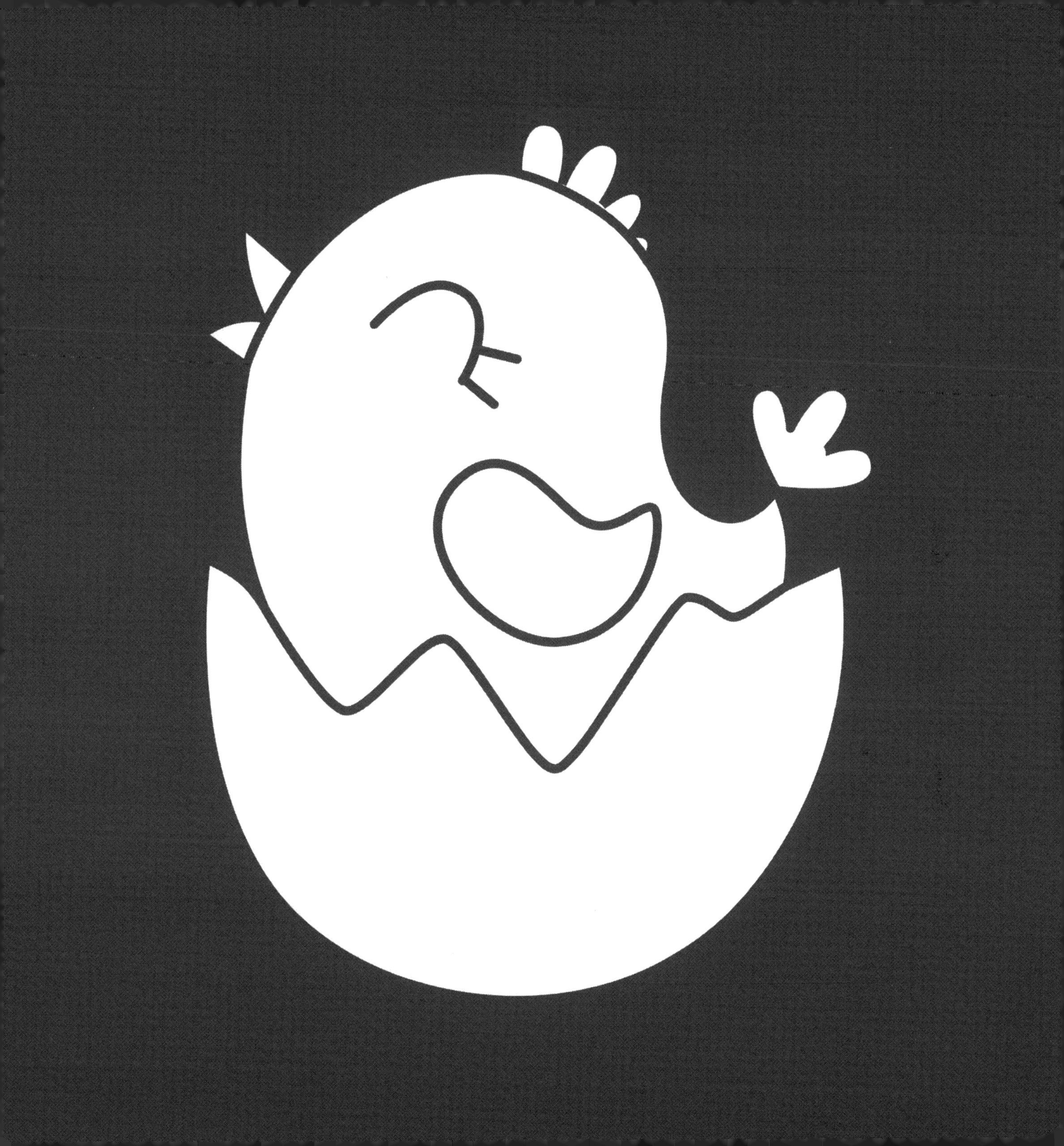

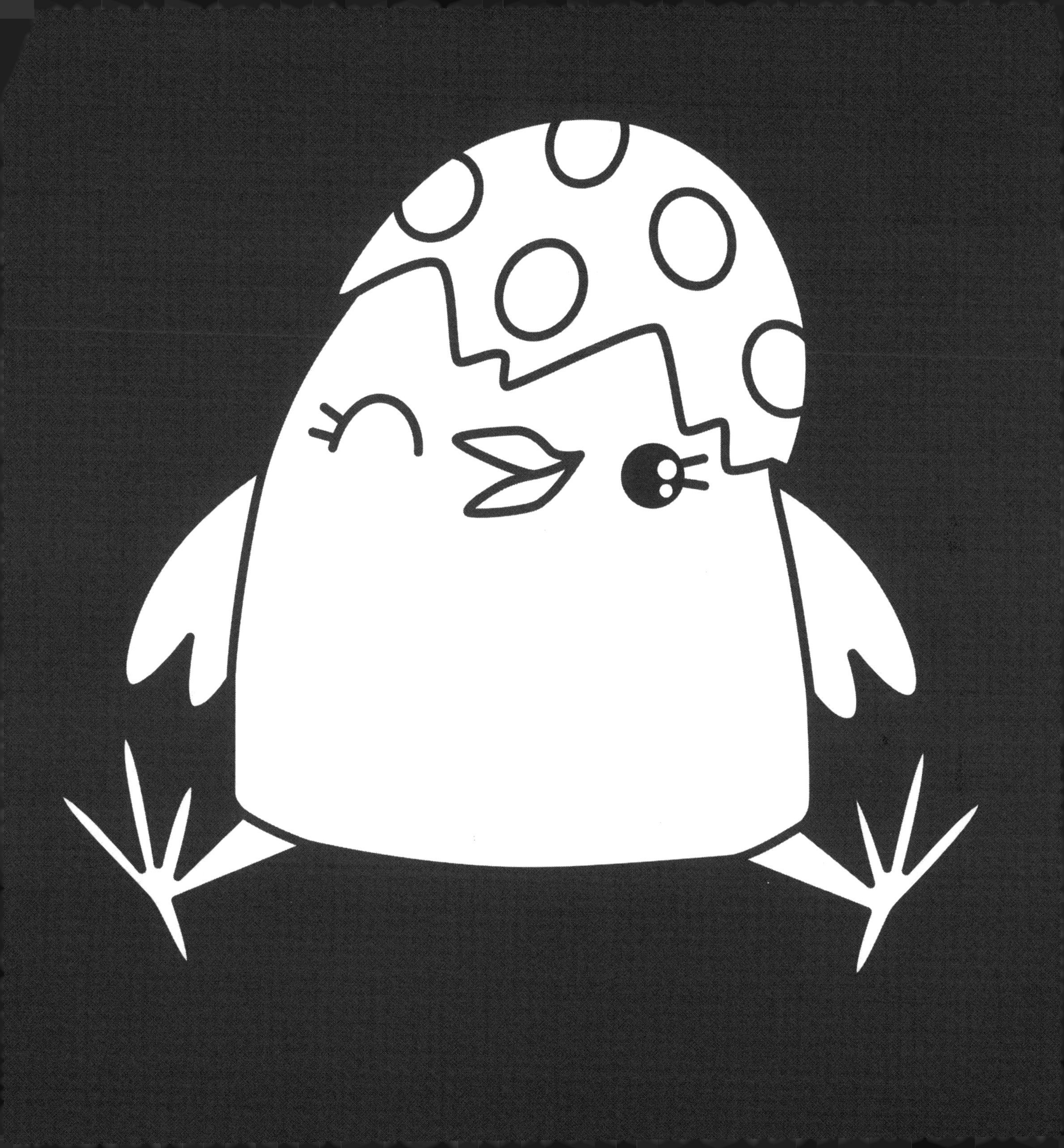

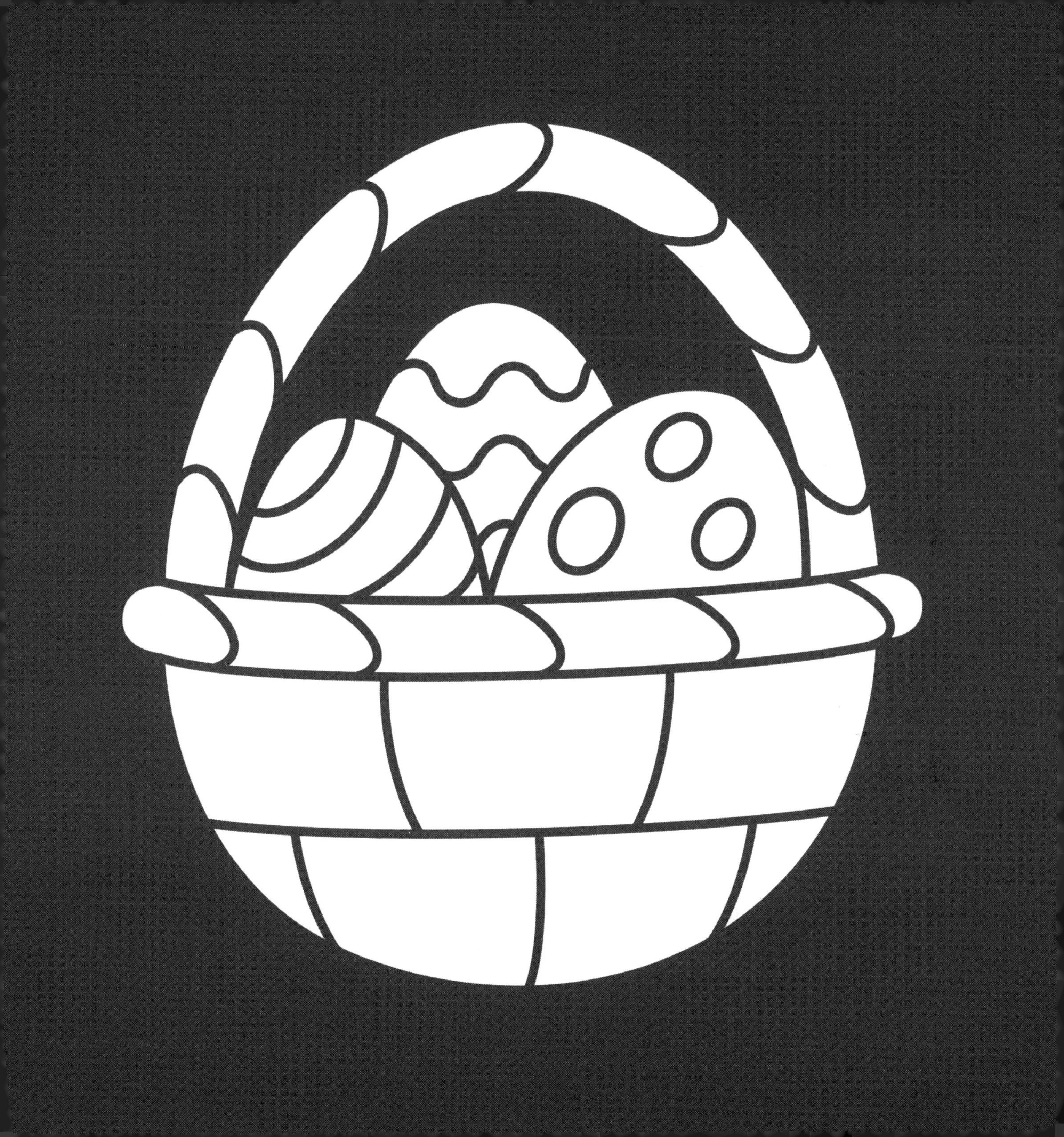

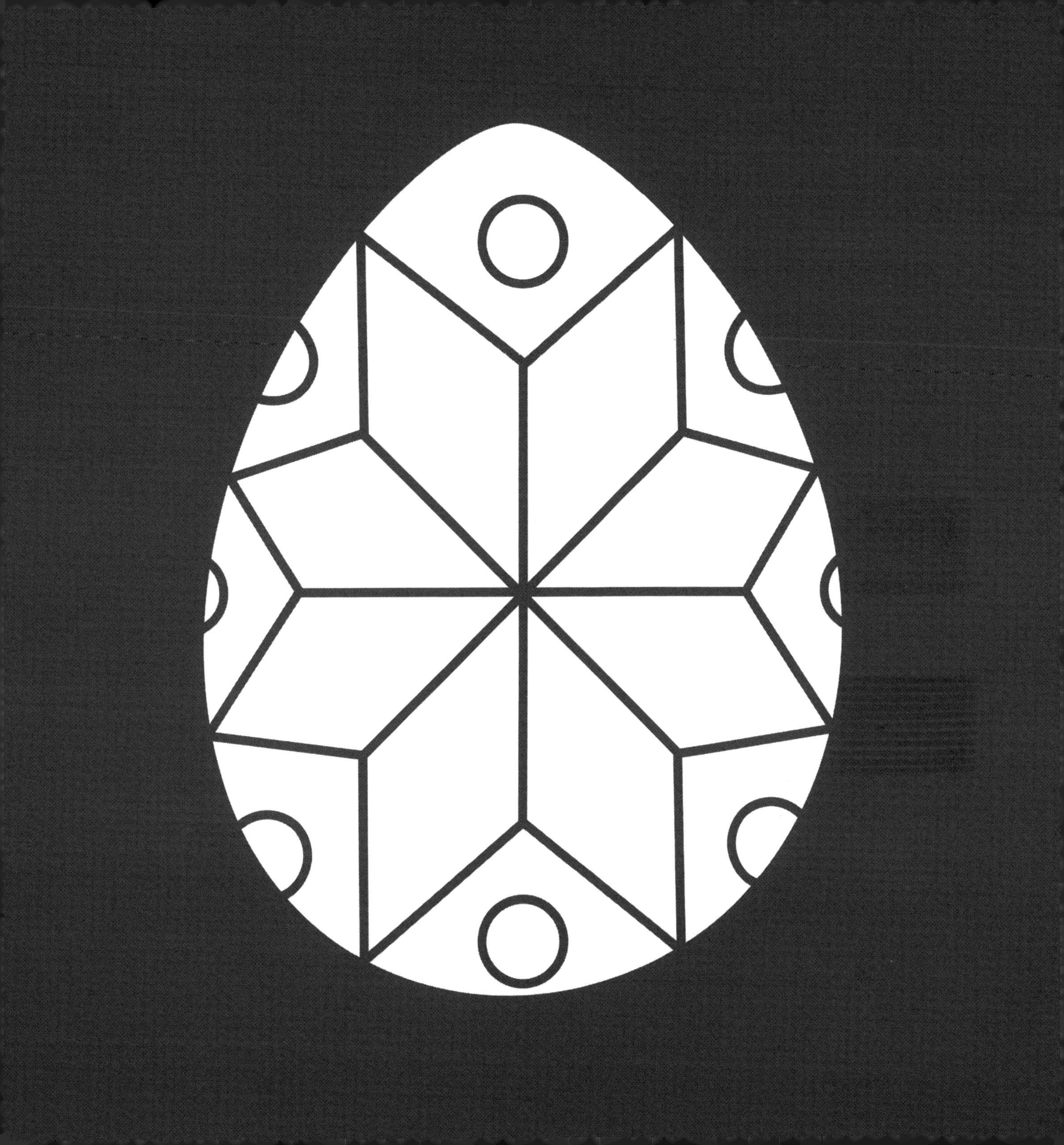

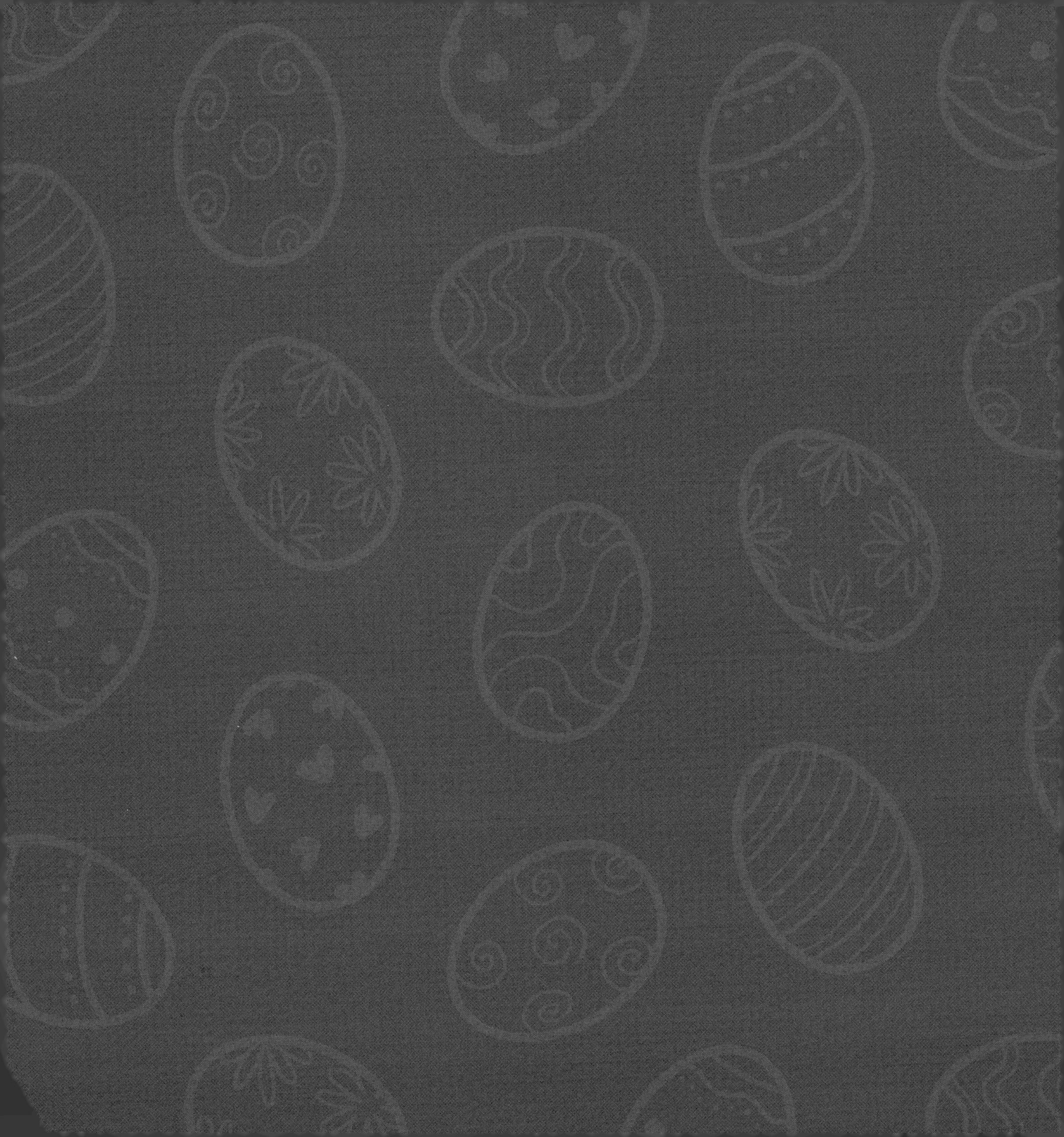

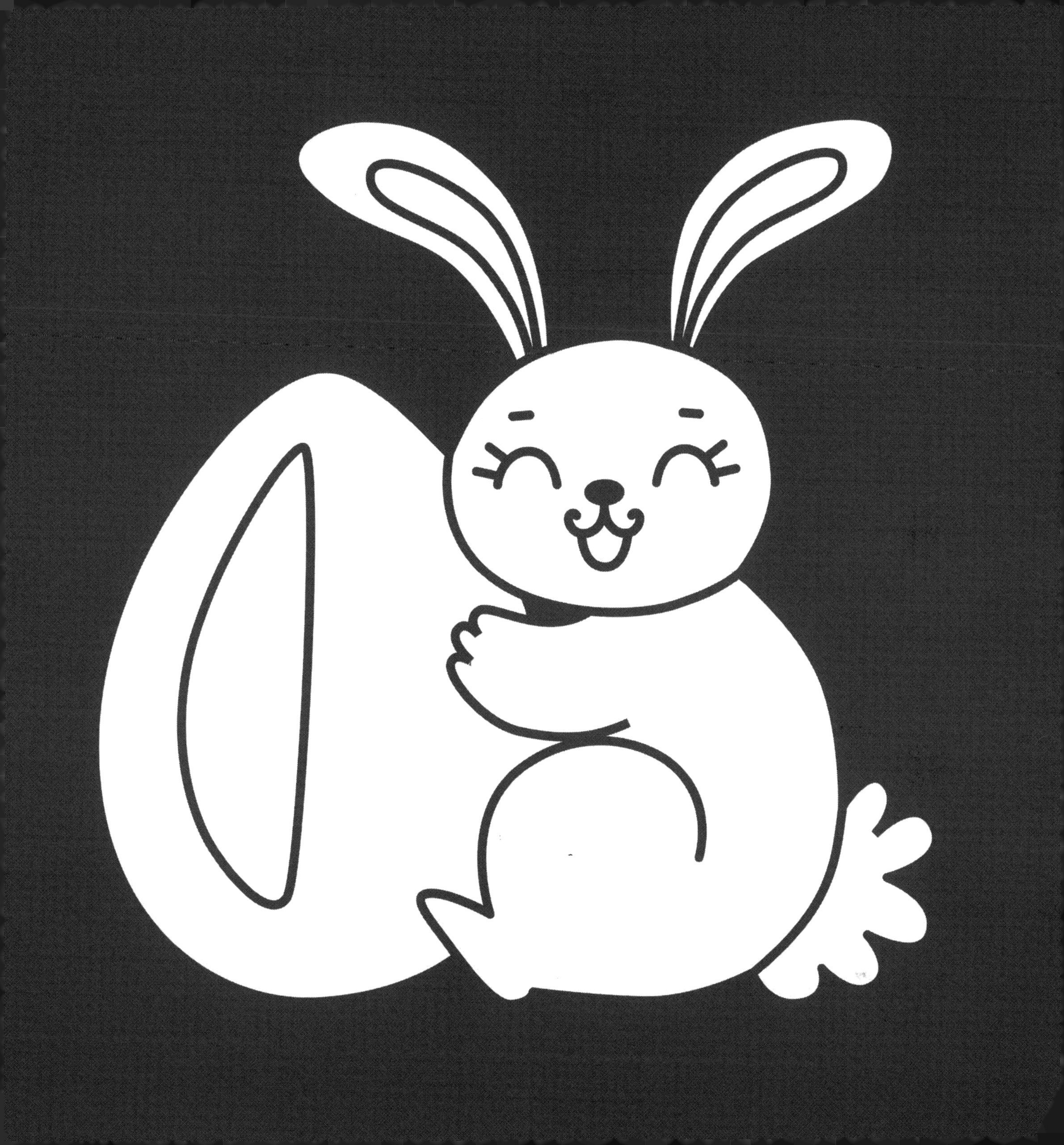

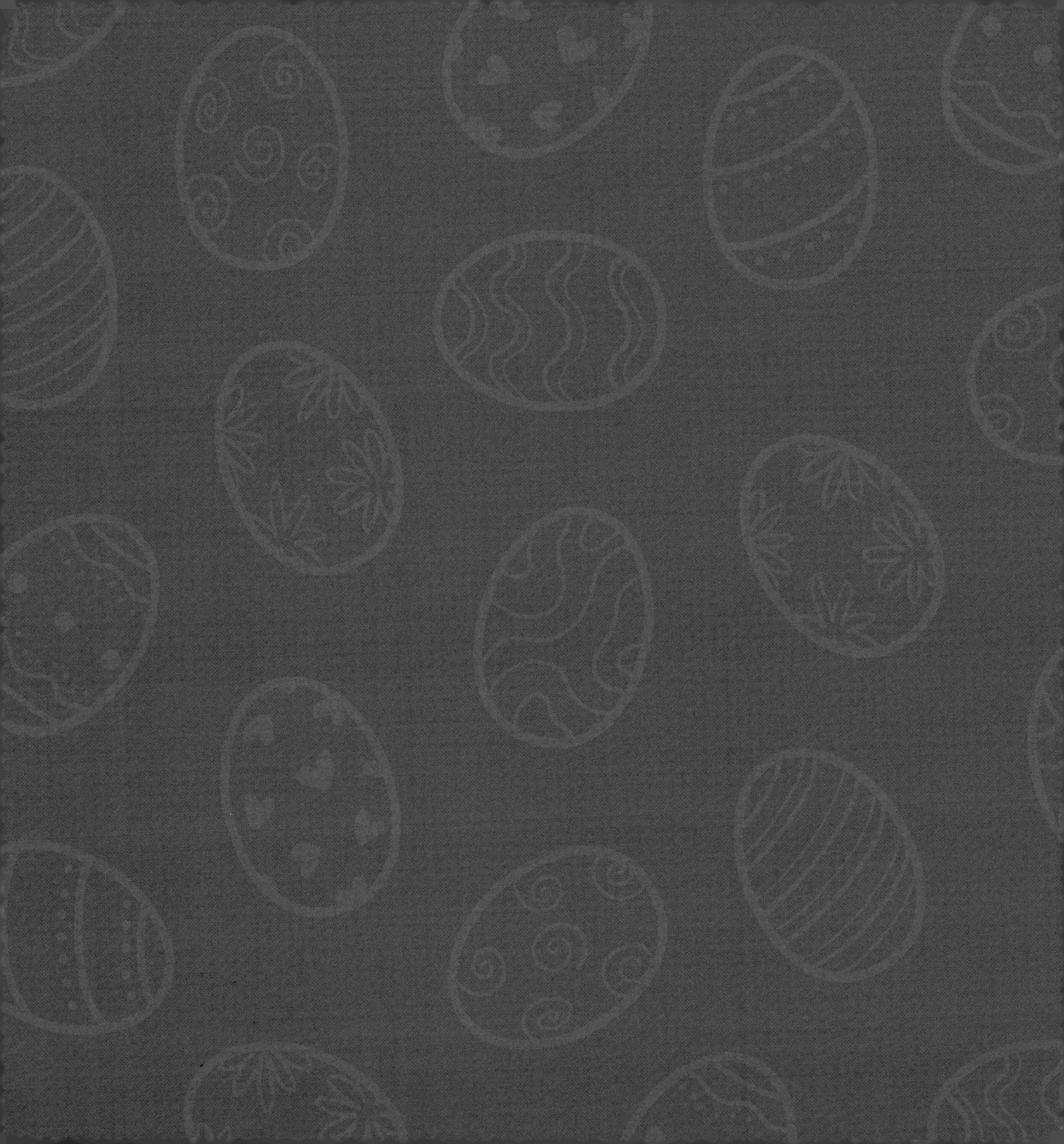

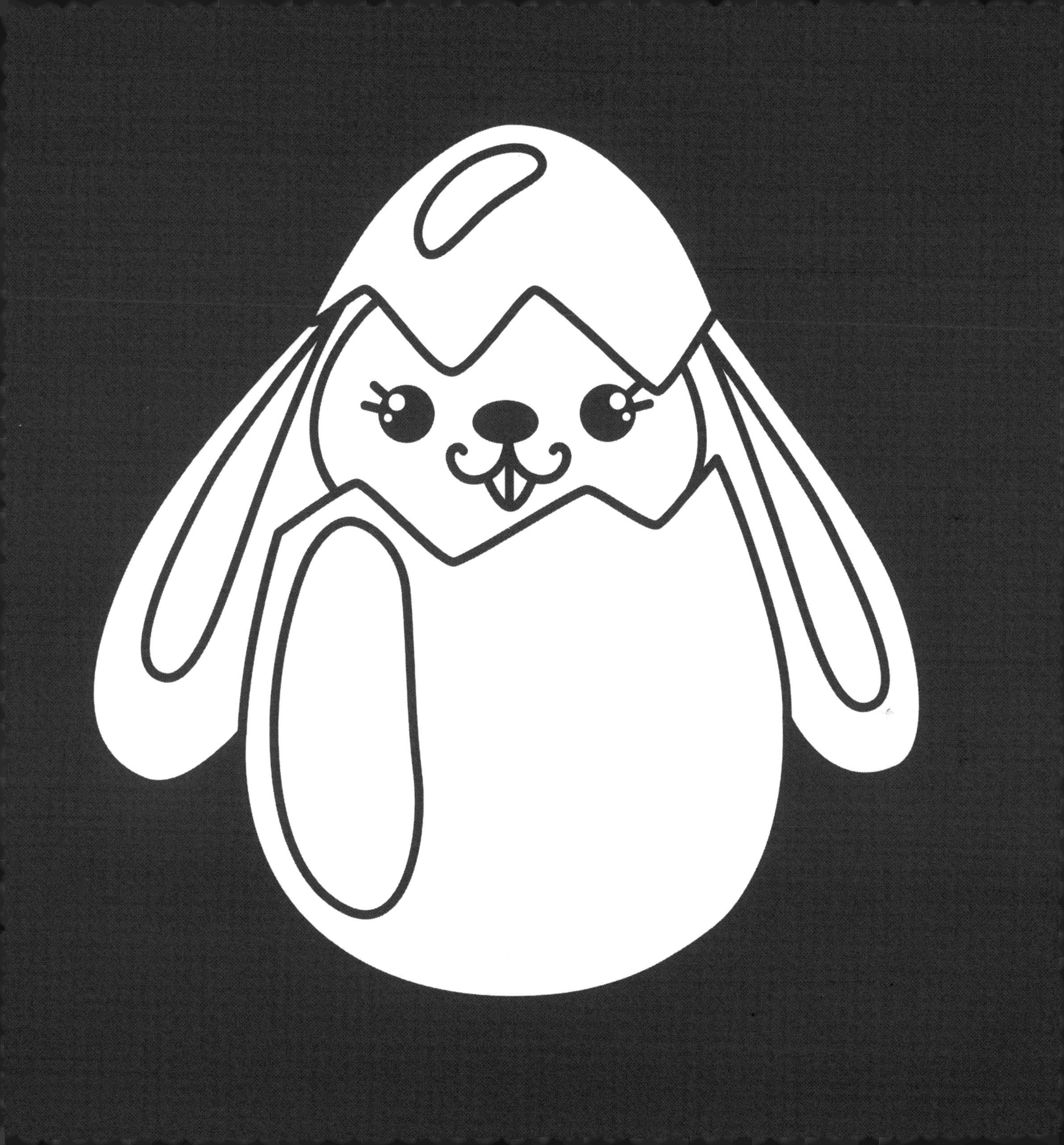

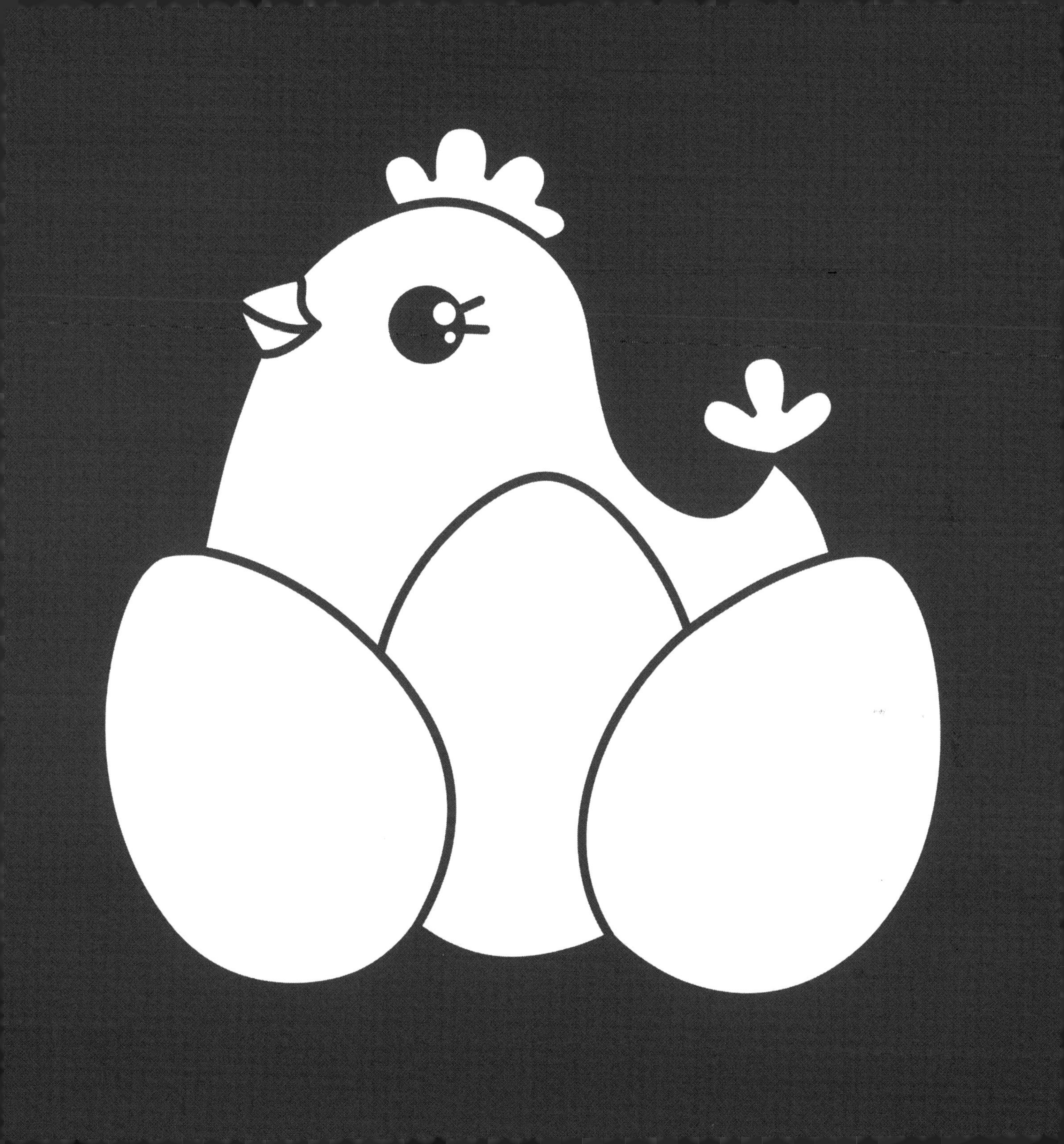

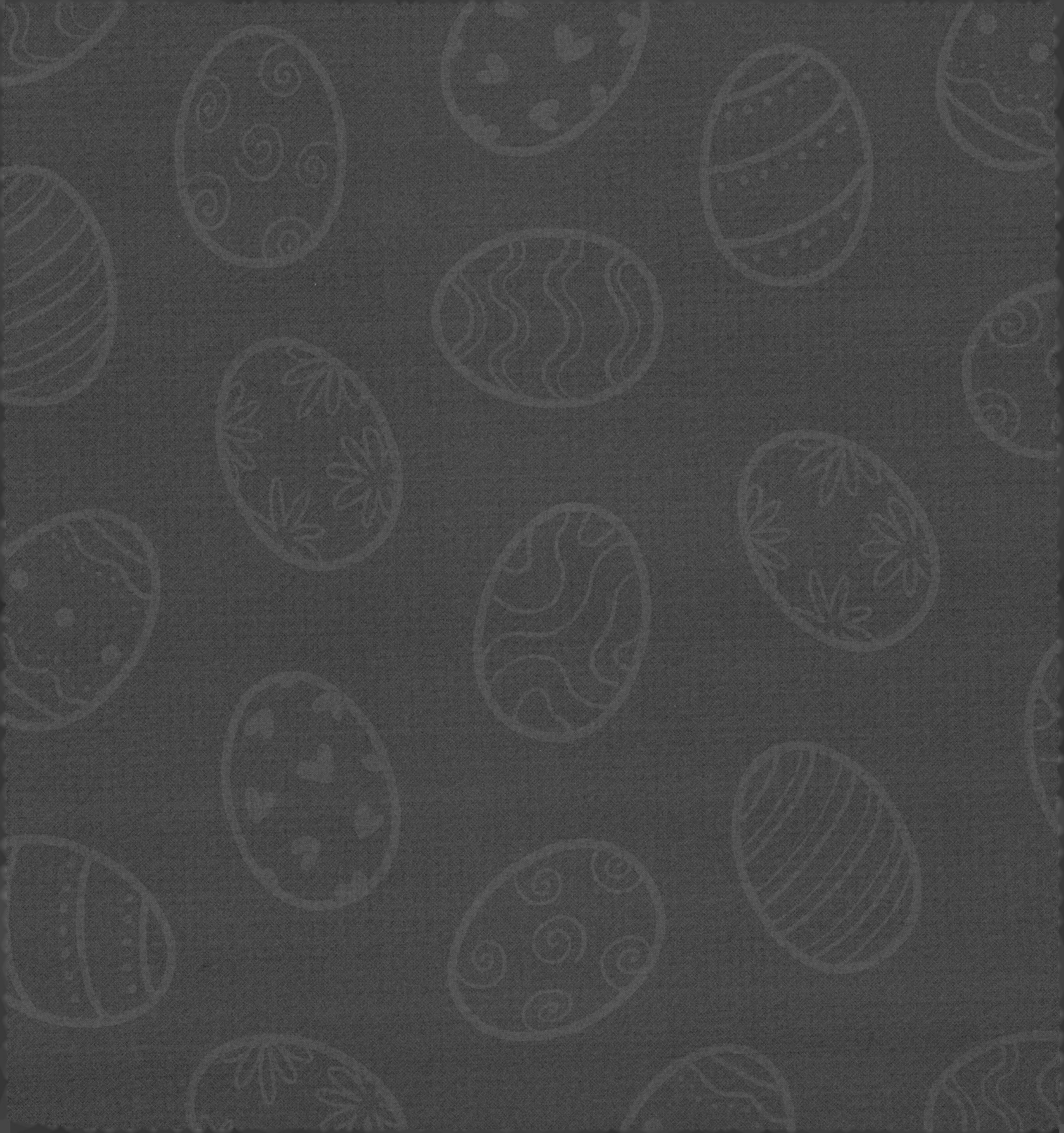

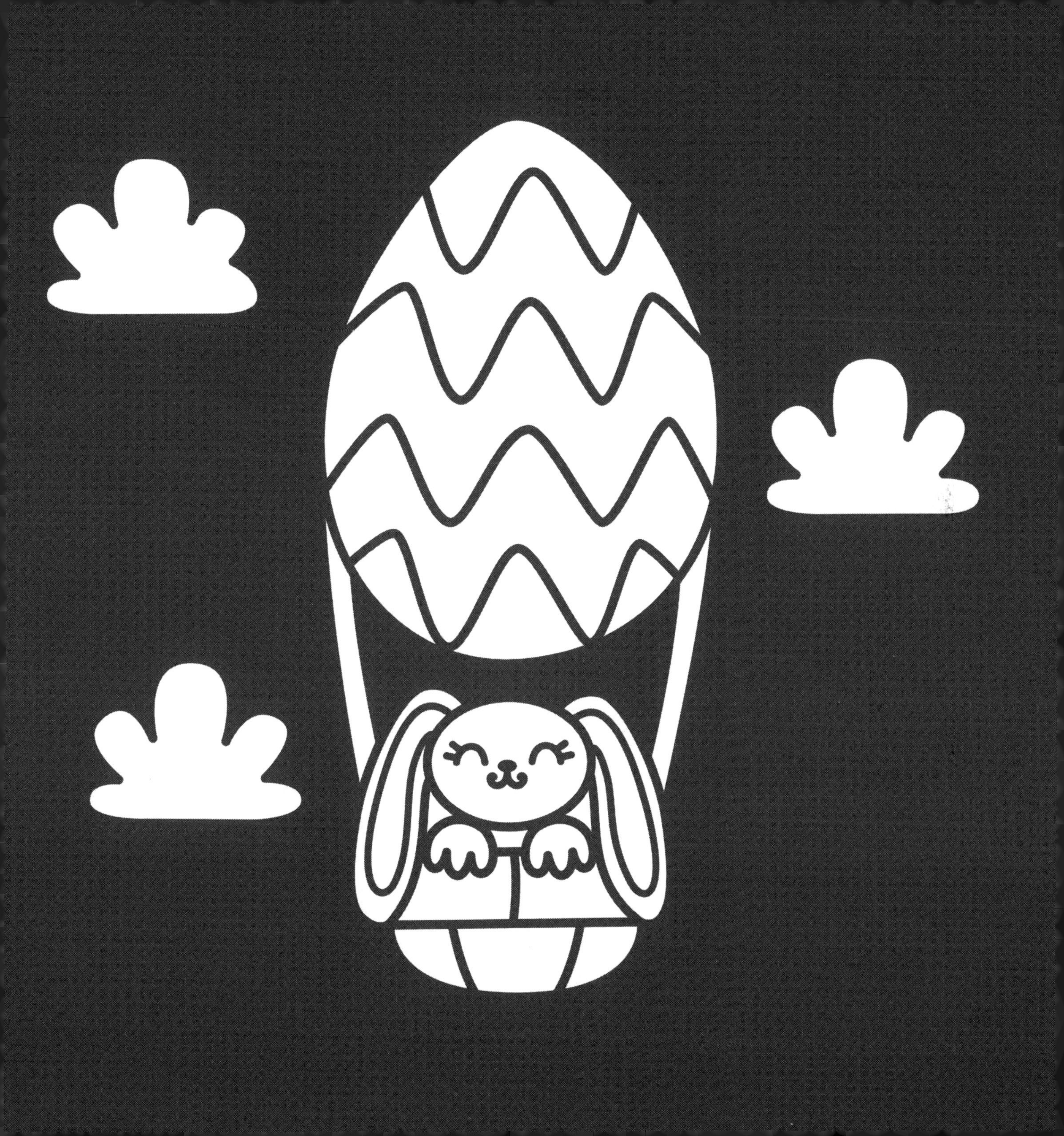

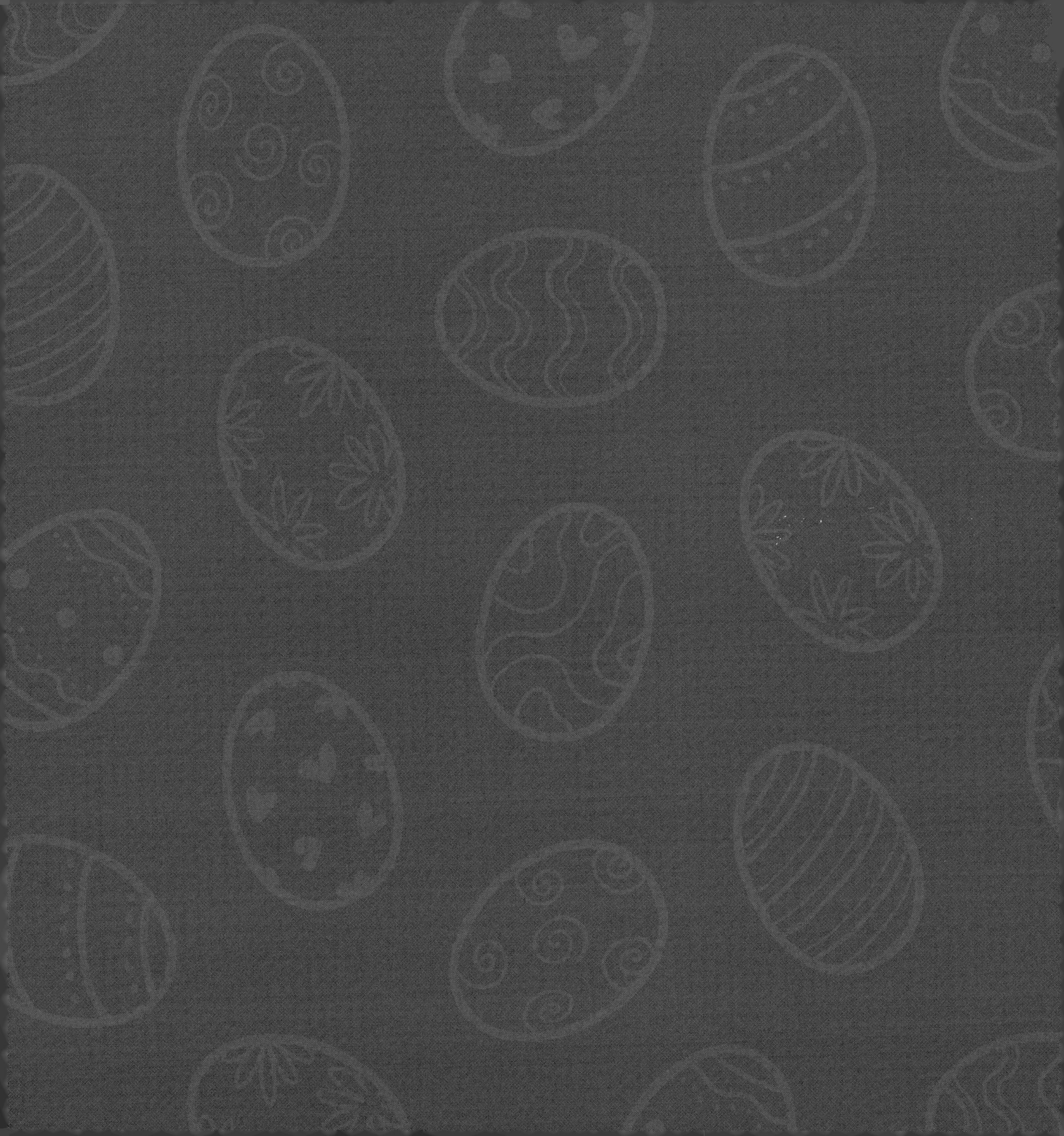

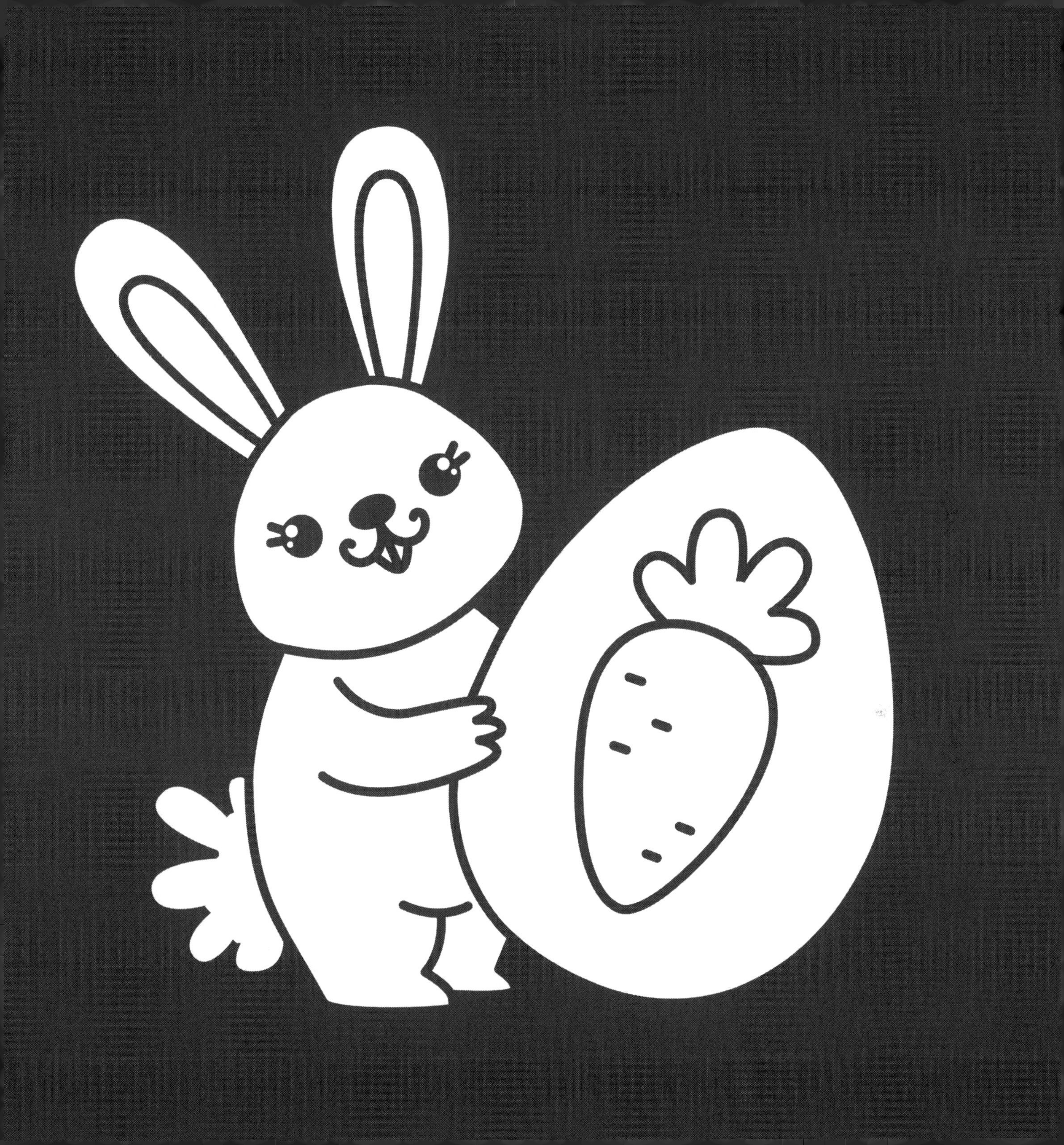

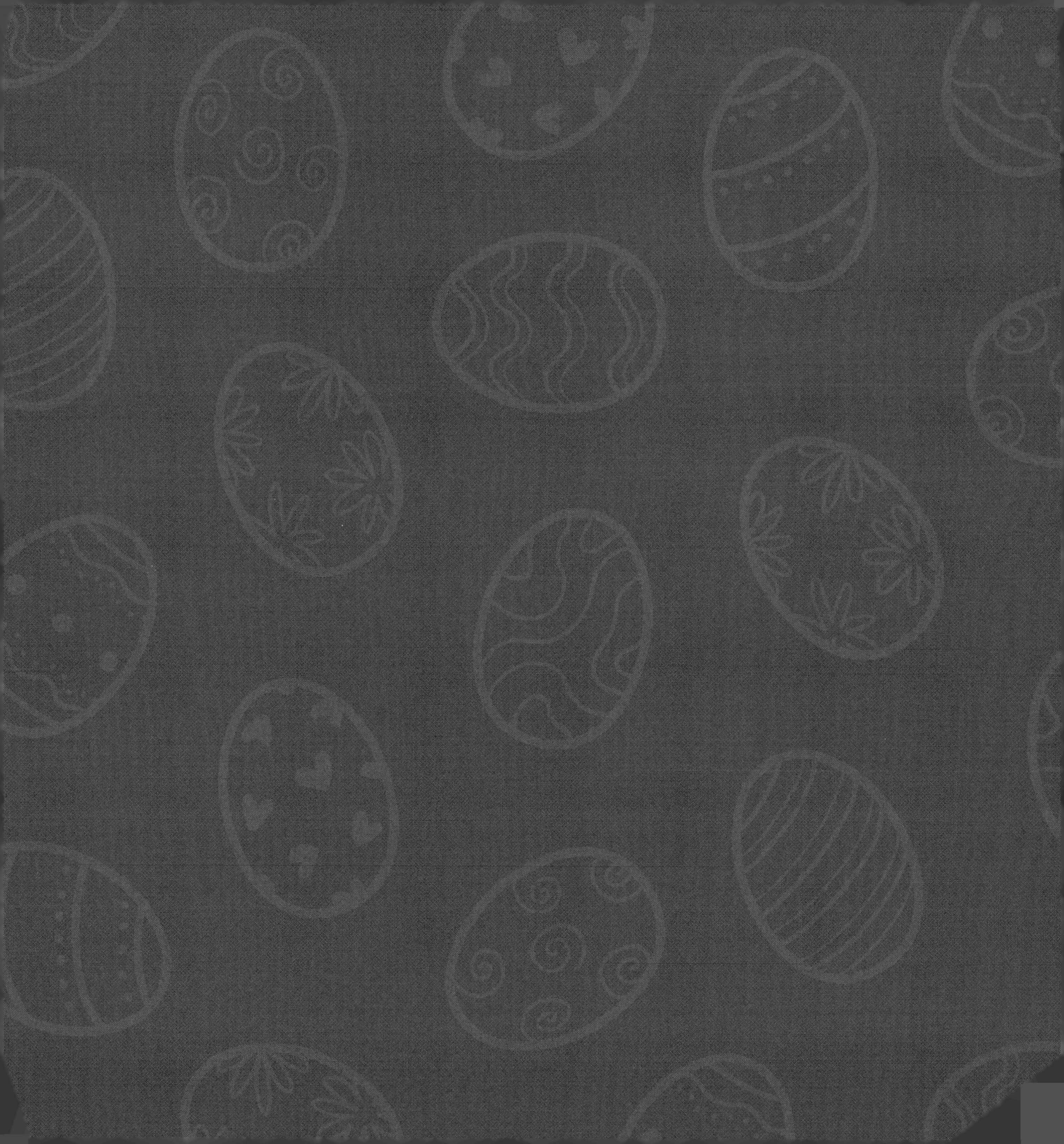

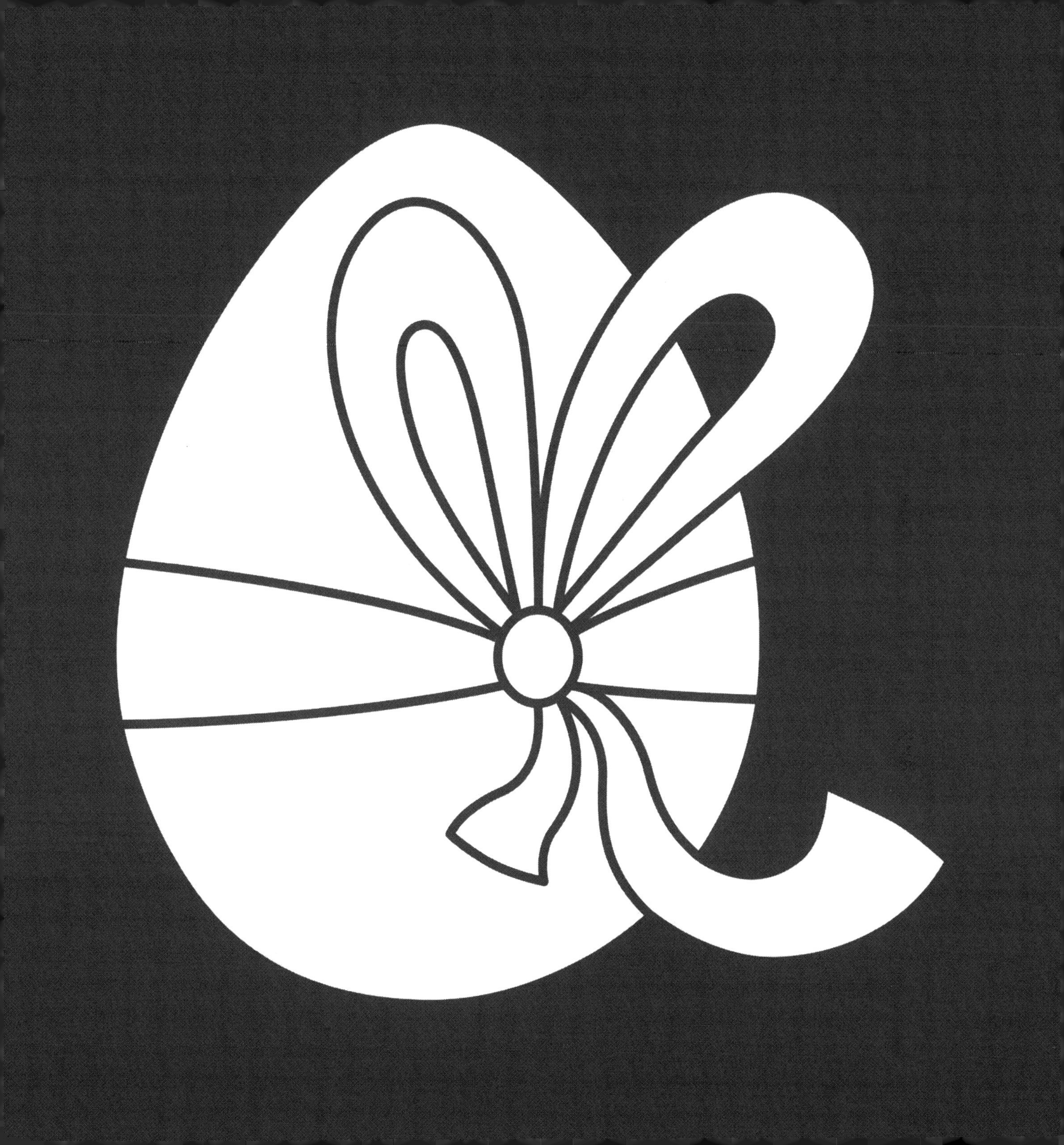

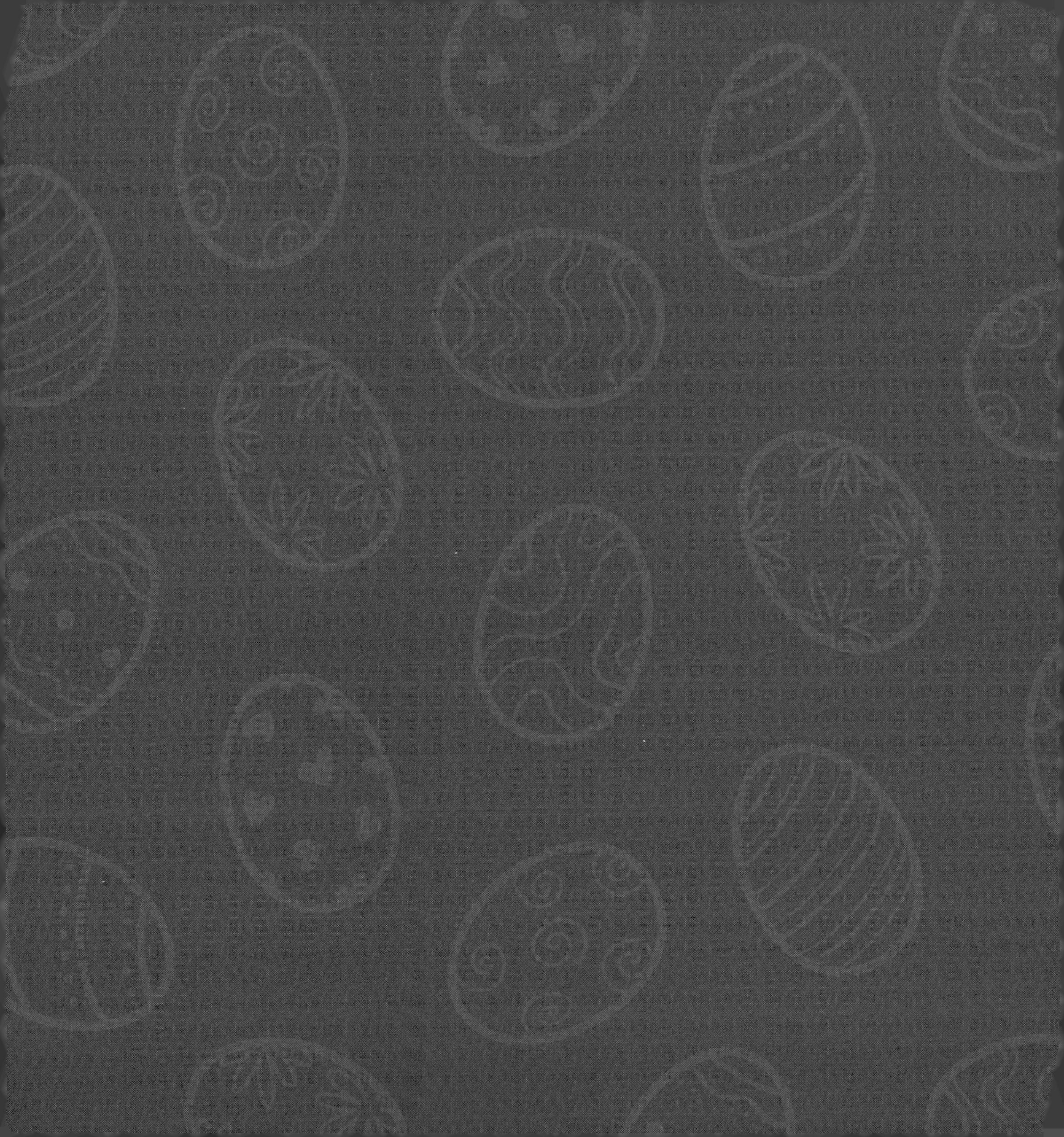

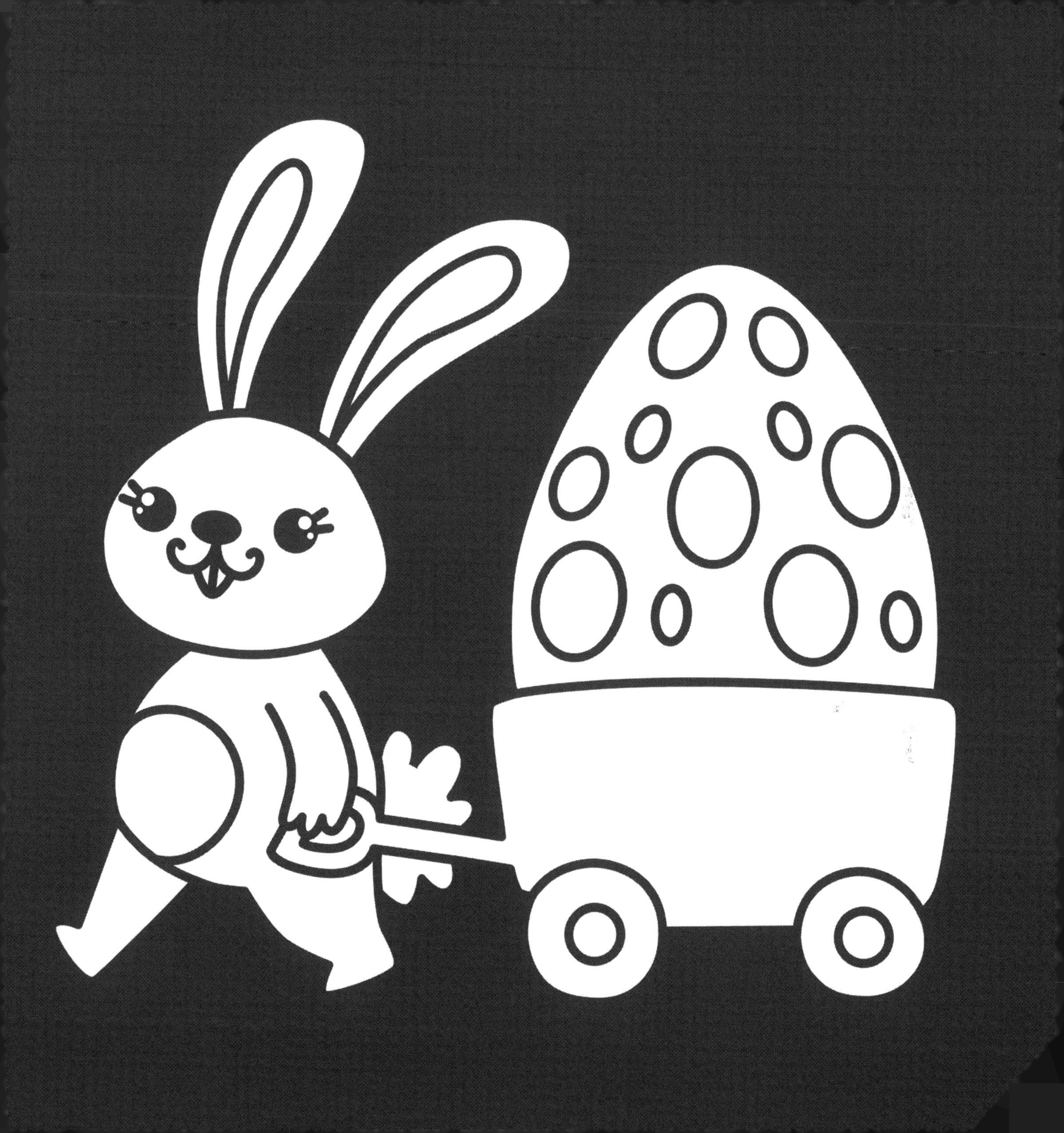

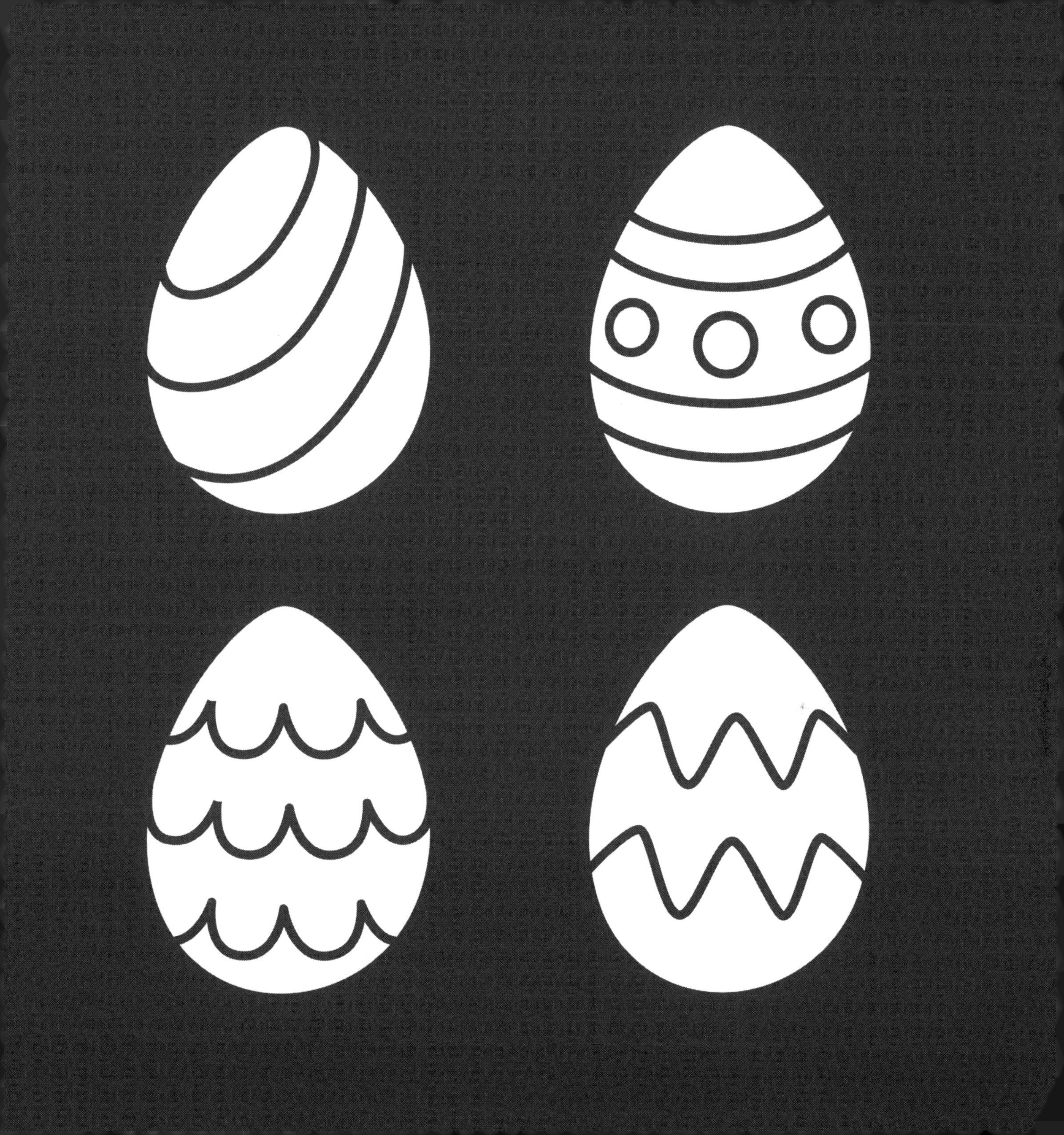

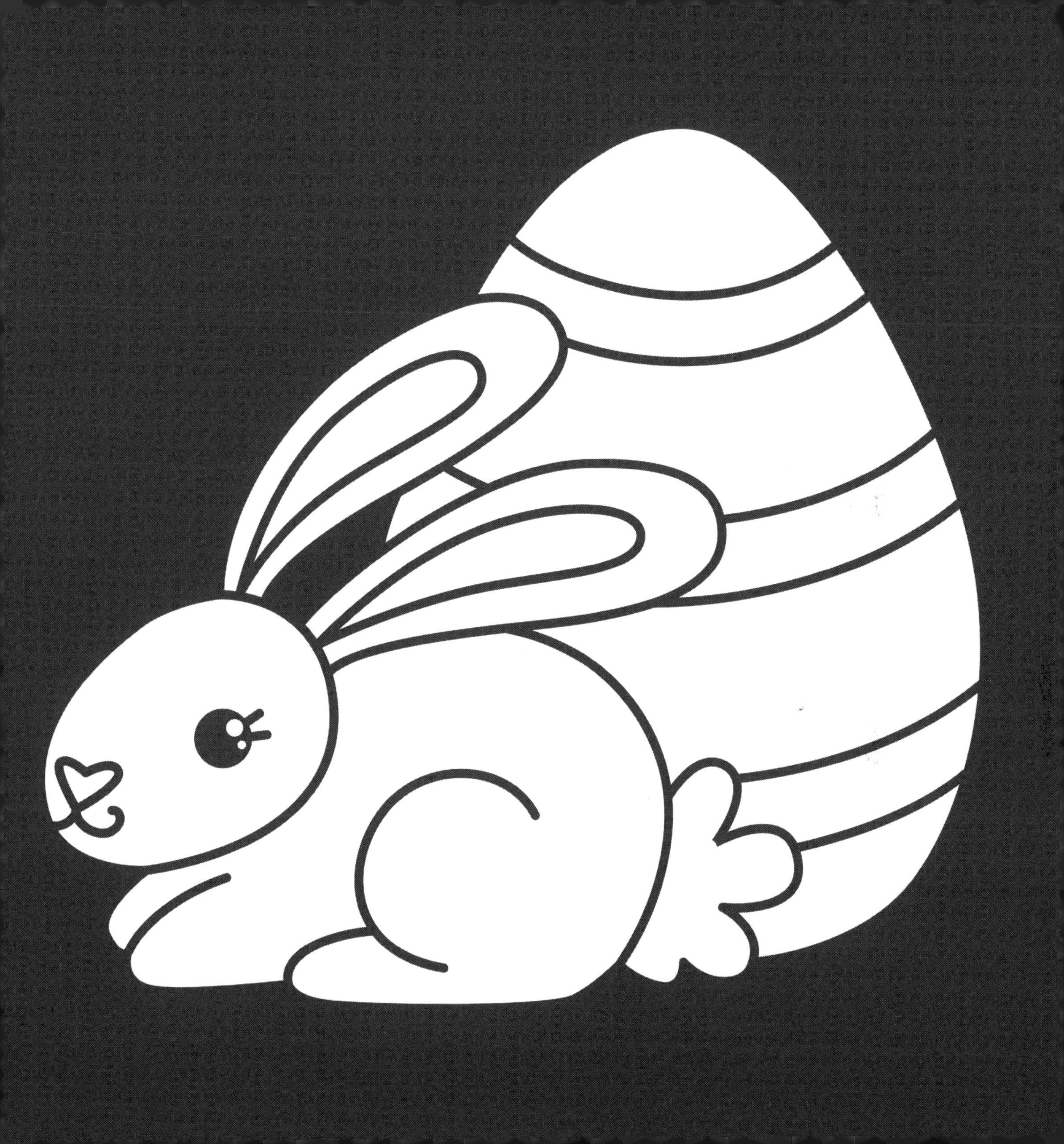

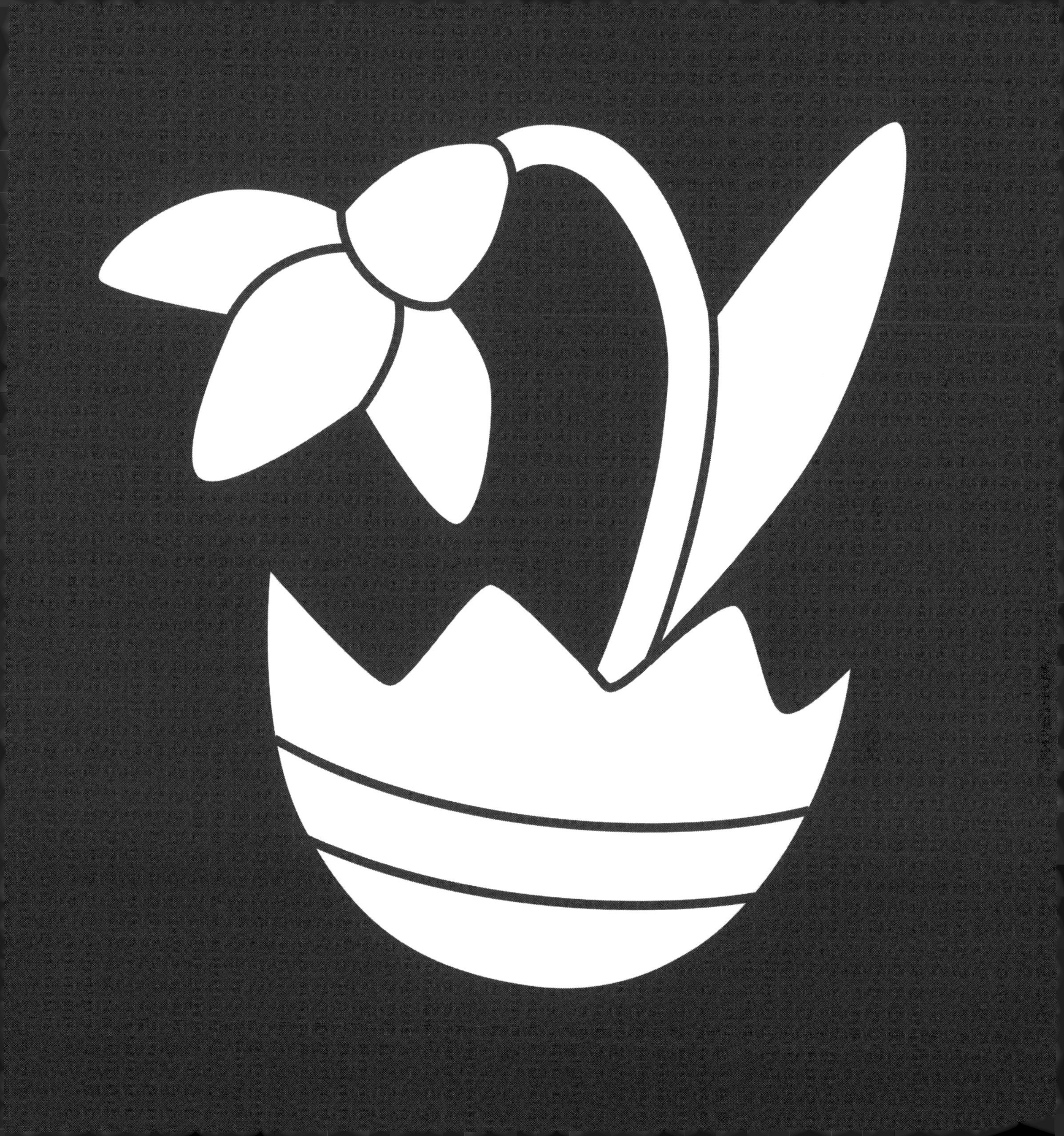

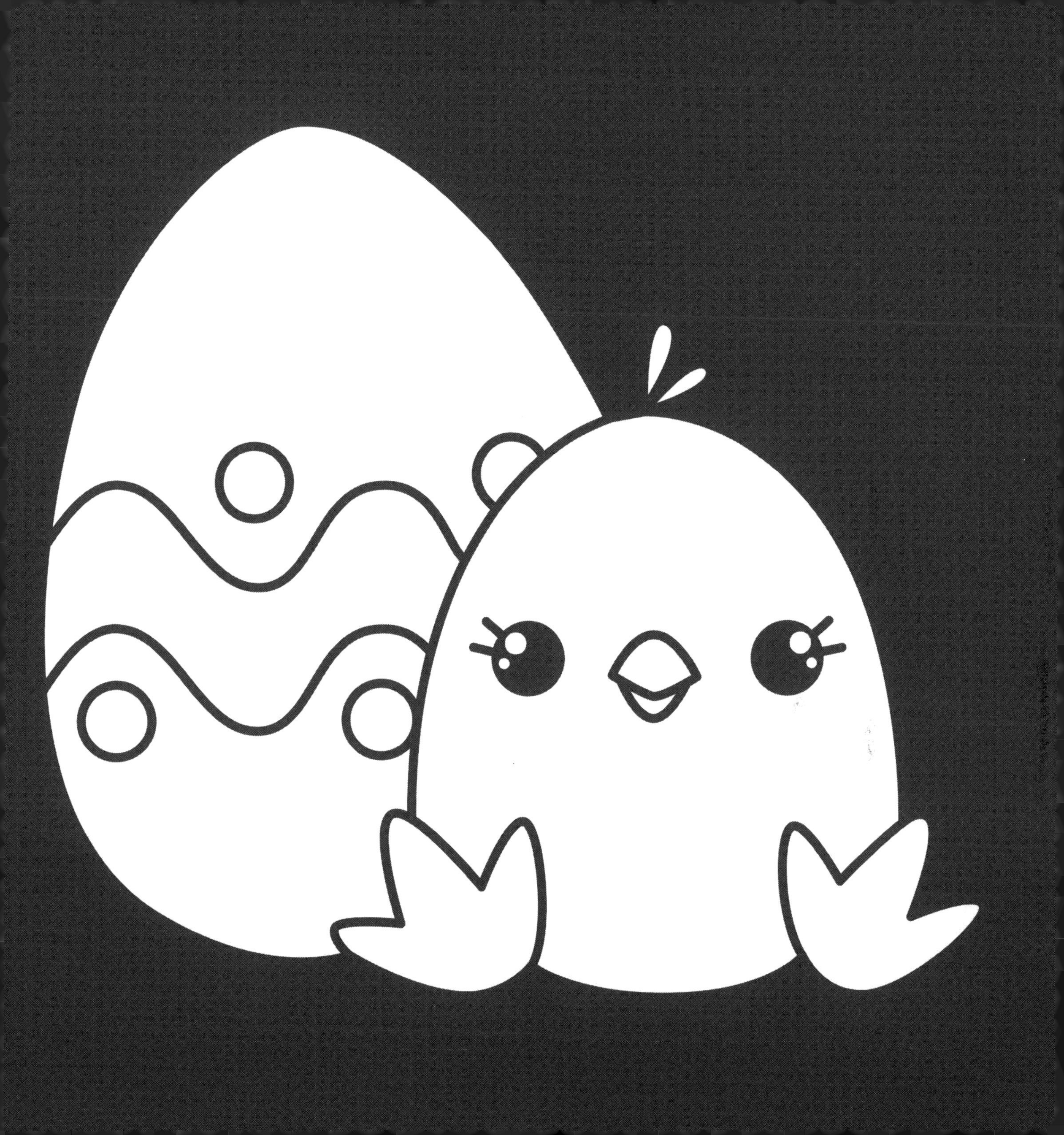

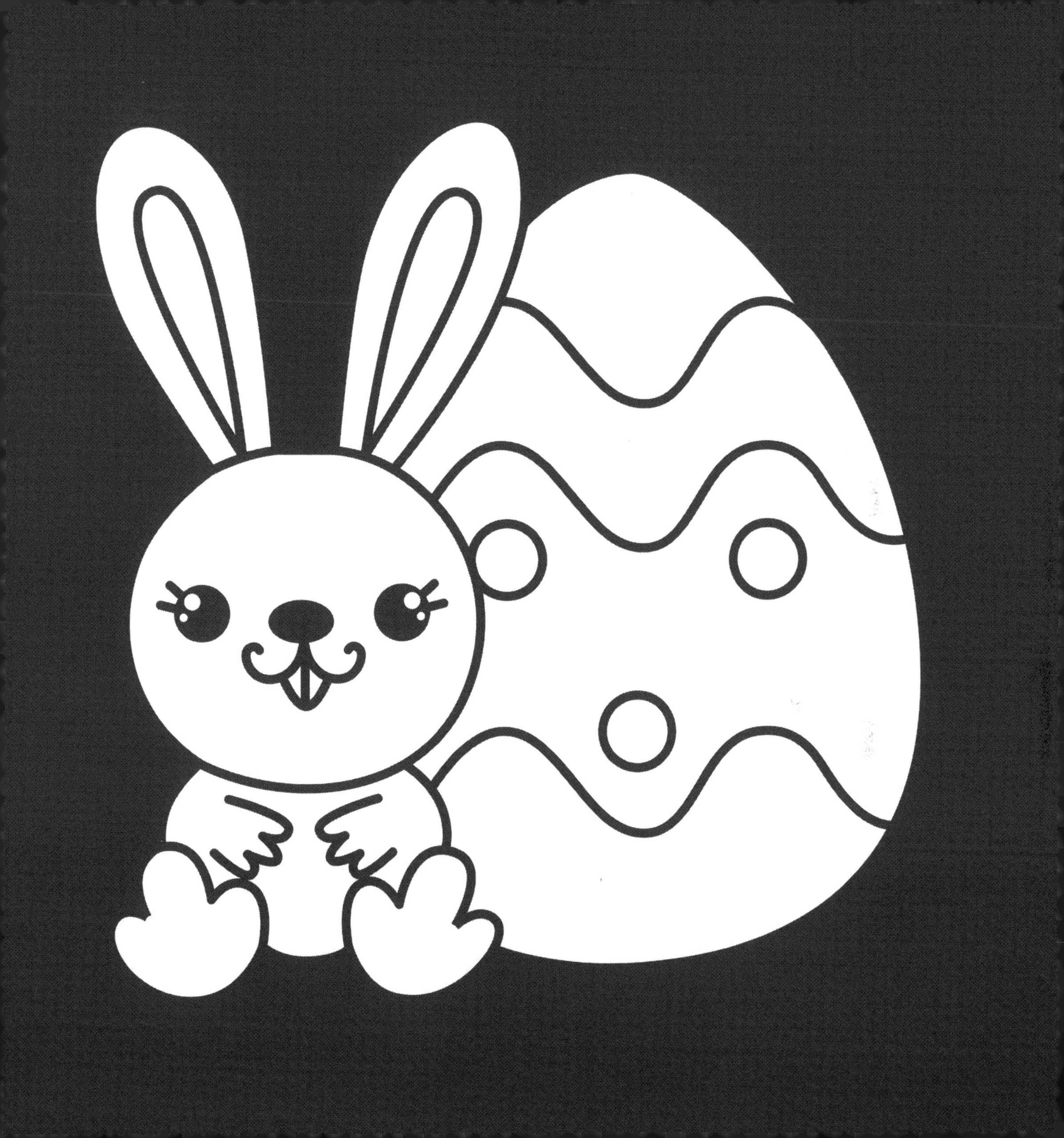

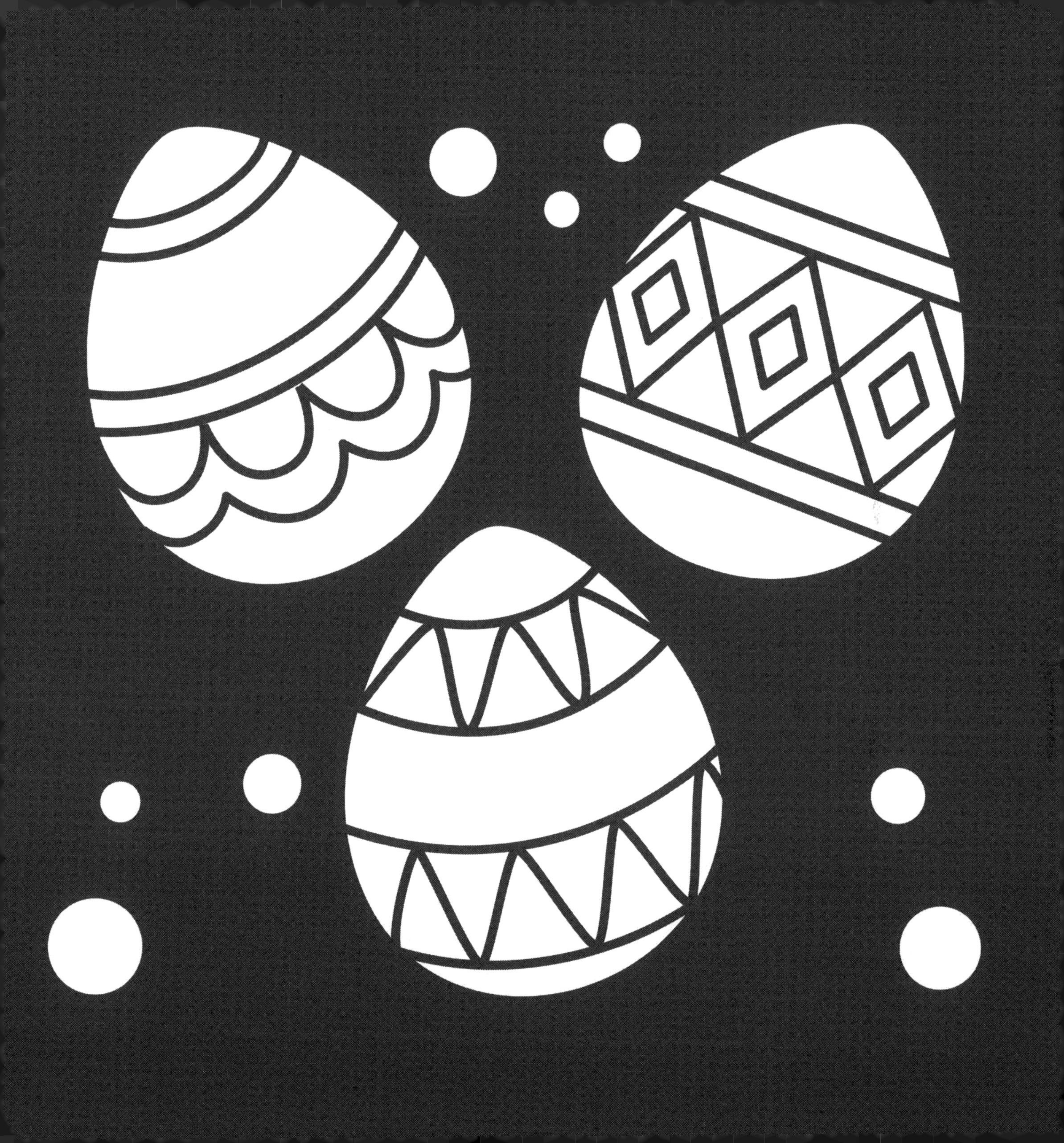

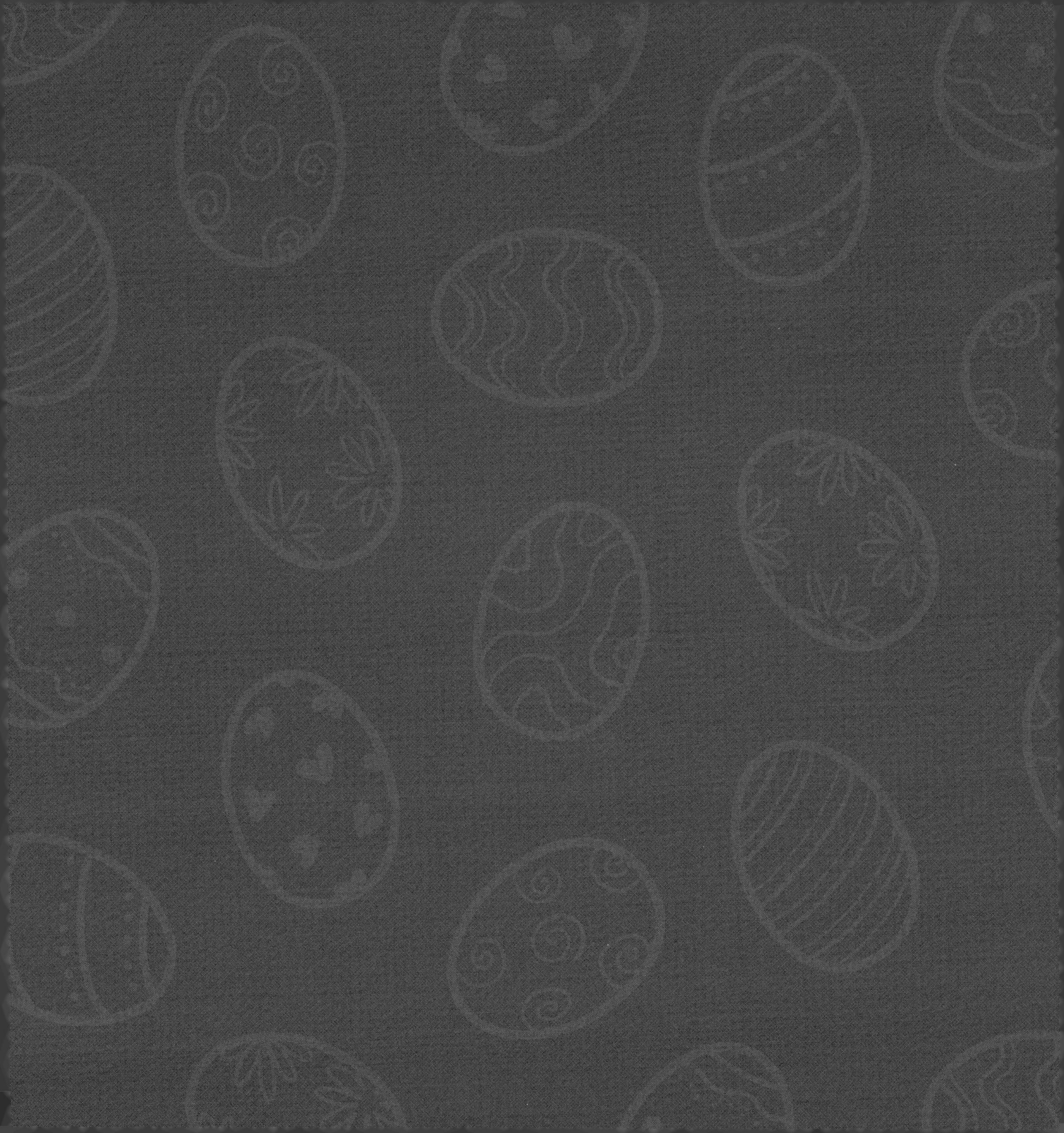

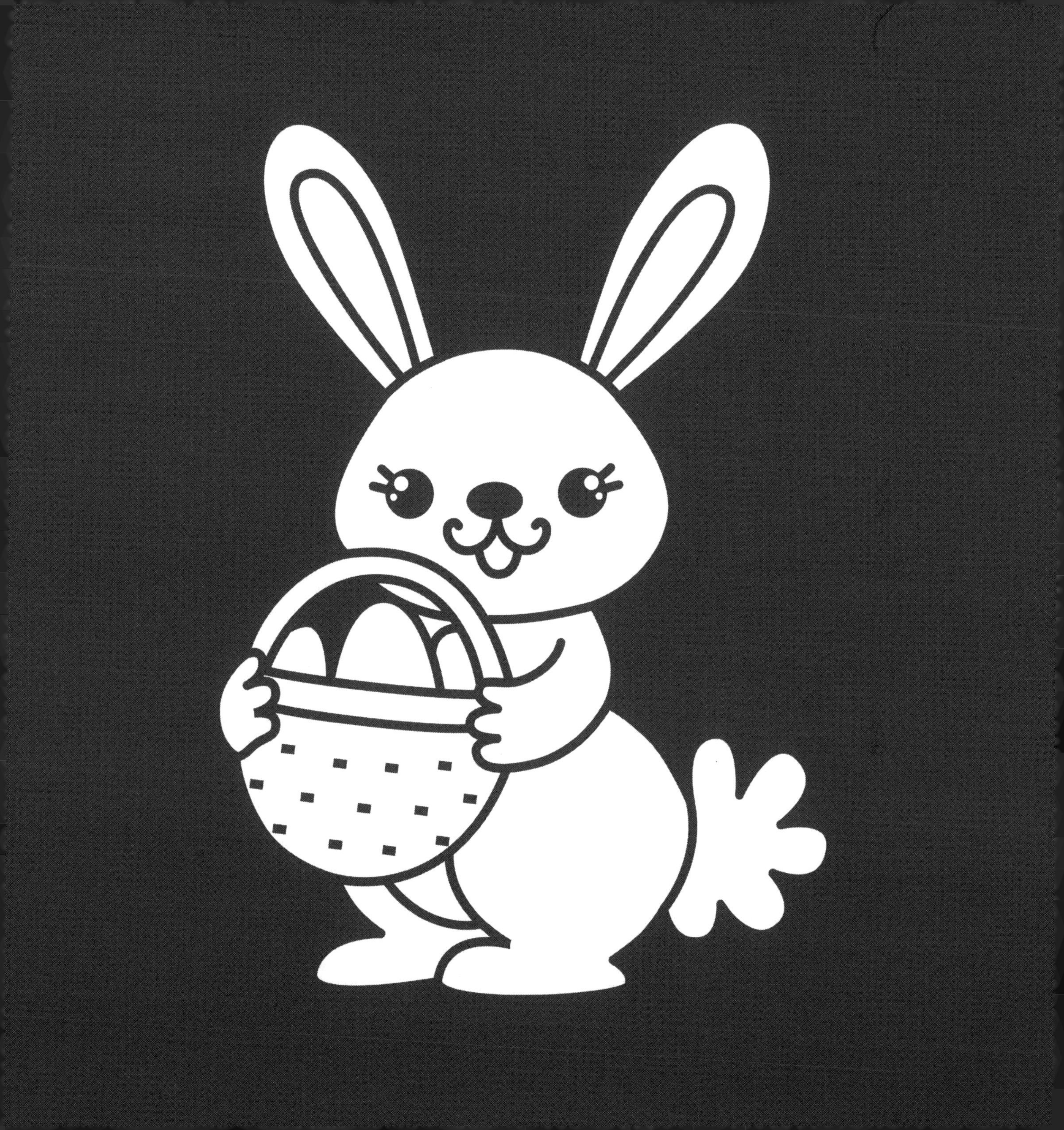

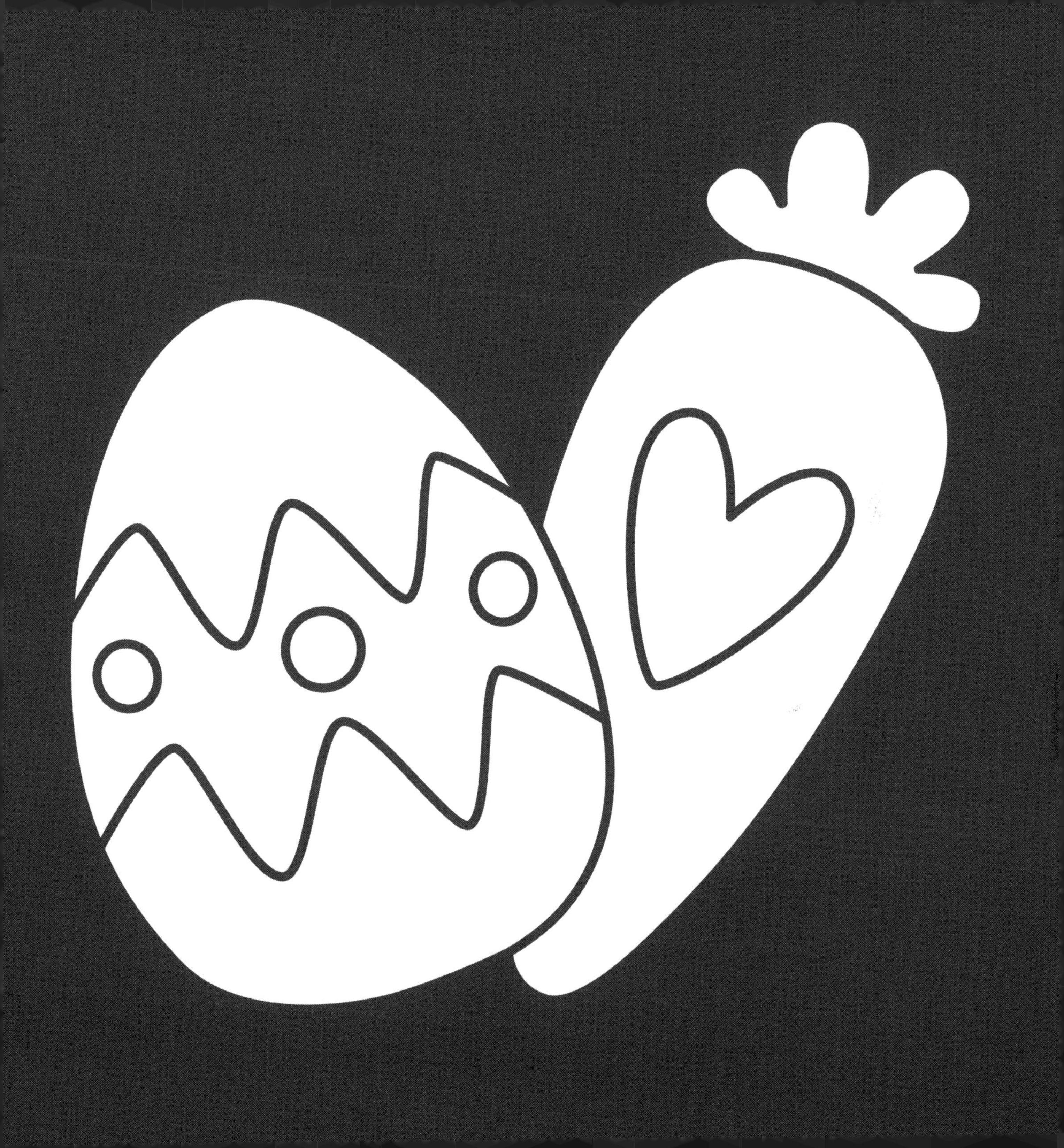

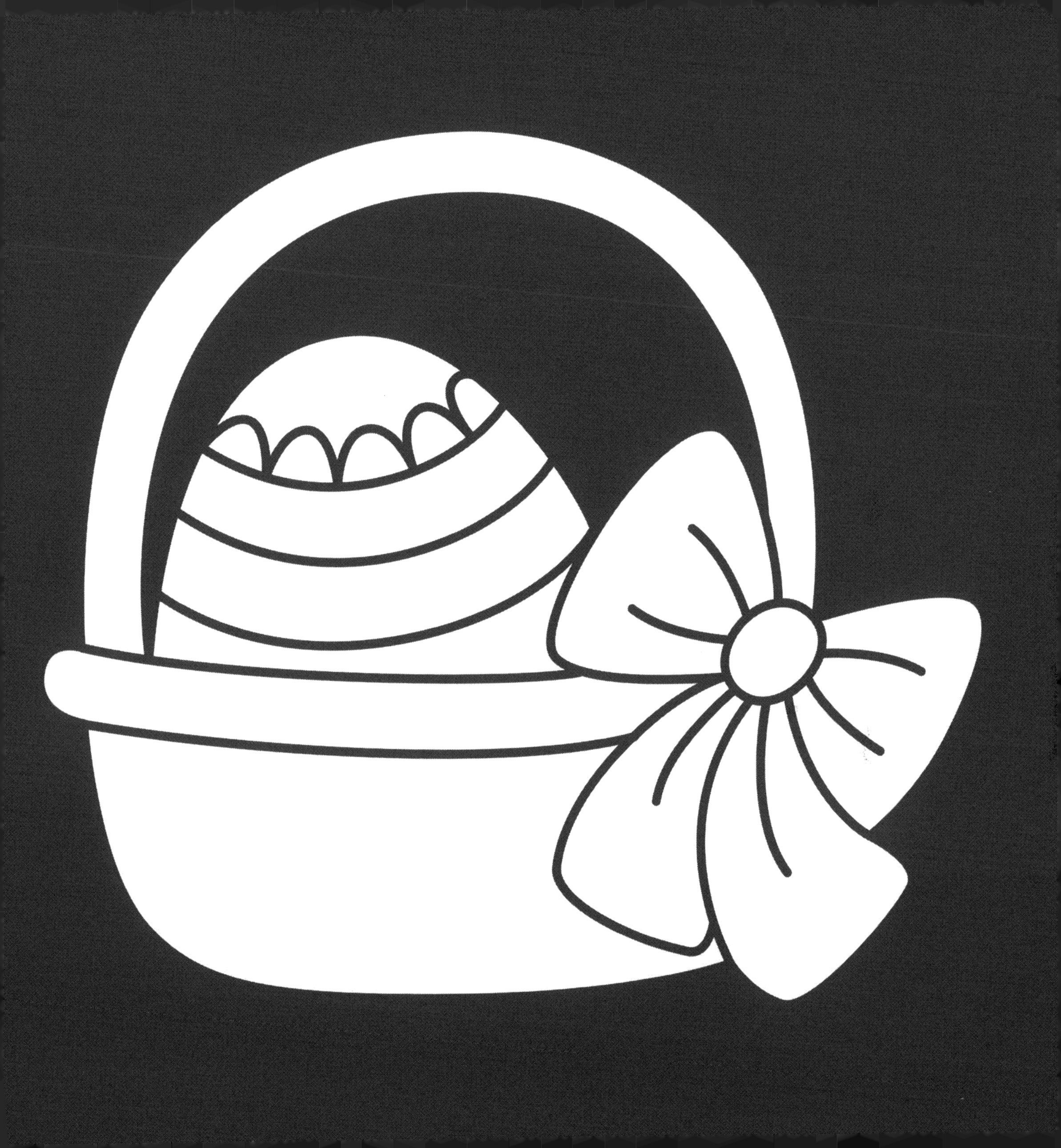

Font used for creation of the cover: Abyss typefacedio
studiofago.com

Made in the USA
Columbia, SC
25 February 2023

12974084R00039